CONTENTS

ACKNOWLEDGEMENTS

Warmest thanks are due to Professor Trevor Dannatt, who over the years has generously given his time and energies towards organising a tribute to Wells Coates. Without his efforts neither this volume nor the travelling exhibition would have come about. The Wells Coates Exhibition Committee are much indebted to Sherban Cantacuzino for allowing them to draw freely on his book *Wells Coates: A Monograph*, and for his encouragement in other ways. They also thank Jane Drew, Maxwell Fry, Alan Irvine, Sir James Richards and all those involved in discussions and schemes at earlier stages.

The photographs and drawings in the exhibition and in this volume are largely drawn from the collection of Wells Coates's daughter, Mrs Laura Cohn; the remainder are the copyright of *The Architectural Review* or the RIBA Drawings Collection.

Thanks are also extended to the Arts Council of Great Britain, the Museum of Modern Art Oxford, the Victoria and Albert Museum, Randal Bell, Patrick Gwynne, Pierre Macke, Ray Norton, Iradj Parvaneh, Richard Tymons, Margaret O'Brien, Sue Sturges, and all the students and staff in Architecture and Publishing at Oxford Polytechnic who have contributed in different ways.

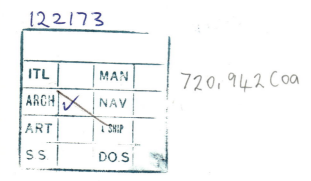

WELLS COATES

Architect and Designer 1895 — 1958

WELLS COATES

Architect and Designer 1895 — 1958

First published 1979 by Oxford Polytechnic Press, Headington, Oxford OX3 0BP for the Wells Coates Exhibition Committee, Oxford Polytechnic

Printed and bound by Cotswold Press, Ferry Hinksey Road, Oxford

© Oxford Polytechnic Press 1979

ISBN 0 902692 22 4

General editor	Laura Cohn
Architectural editor	Andrew Ozanne
House editors	Charmian Cliff Hodges, Richard Powell
Designer	Debbie Mabey

Poster design	Kevin Hemmings
Exhibition architects	Kevin Hemmings, Andrew Ozanne, David Tonkinson
Architectural advisers	Ian Davis, Stuart Lewis, Paul Oliver, Tom Porter
Typographic advisers	Tom Colverson, Dennis Hall, Jamie Maughan
Photography	Iradj Parvaneh, John Austin
Exhibition panels	Replicard Ltd, Bavaria Road, London
Exhibition typesetting	Oxford Publishing Services, Stratford Street, Oxford
Photographic printing	Pronda Pronda Ltd, St Clements, Oxford

THE EXHIBITS FOR THE MUSEUM OF MODERN ART, OXFORD

Shorthand diary kept by Wells Coates in Japan, 1911
Wells Coates in a Canadian lumber camp, c. 1915
Wells Coates as a young man with his family
Wells Coates with 2nd Division of Canadian Gunners, France, 1917
   (standing next to horse)
Wells Coates c. 1924
Radio Times 20 May 1932
E. & L. Berg's brochures for the Sunspan House designed in 1934
Brochure for Embassy Court Flats, Brighton, 1934
Programme for the 5th Congress of Les Congrès Internationaux
   d'Architecture Moderne (CIAM), 1937
The MARS (Modern Architectural Research) Group catalogue for their
   first exhibition at New Burlington Galleries, June 1937
The MARS Group catalogue for 'New Architecture', an exhibition at New
   Burlington Galleries, 11-29 January 1938
Ideal Home Vol. LIII No. VI June 1946, featuring 'The Homewood', Esher
   in the article 'Freedom from Convention in Planning'
Page from Wells Coates's Report on Room Units, April 1947
'La Charte de l'Habitat': copy of drawing given by Wells Coates to
   Le Corbusier, winner of the RIBA Gold Medal, 1953
Four of Coates's crayon sketches for his Vancouver Flats project, 1957

Isotype Dwelling DB4GM: perspective drawing, pencil and watercolour
Isotype Dwelling SA3.5G: perspective drawings, elevations, and plan,
   pencil and watercolour
Lawn Road Flats: perspective drawing of the garden side, pencil on
   tracing paper
Lawn Road Flats: perspective drawing of the gallery access side facing
   the road, pencil on tracing paper
John Piper: 'Regency Victorian Wells Coates', gouache, 1938
Preliminary studies for the revolutionary Wingsail rig
Coates's Lancia Lambda, drawn by a prospective assistant in 1946
Telekinema at the Festival of Britain: elevation, pencil and water-
   colour

AC85 Ekco wireless, 1934
Thermovent electric fire for Ekco
Coates's first post-war wireless for Ekco, the A22,
   1946
Ekco Radiotime, 1946, combining wireless and alarm

Items exhibited are owned by the British Architectural Library/RIBA,
   Mrs Laura Cohn, Professor Trevor Dannatt, Paul Oliver, and the Victoria
   and Albert Museum

The foundations on which this volume rests are numerous. The earliest were laid twenty-one years ago, when soon after my father's death friends and colleagues in England and Canada proposed some form of memorial and raised money for it. An exhibition, a book, even a sculpture, were discussed. The book — *Wells Coates: A Monograph* — was undertaken by Sherban Cantacuzino; it was published by Gordon Fraser in 1978 and has been welcomed for its fine scholarship and sympathetic yet clear judgement. After its publication Trevor Dannatt wrote to me to say that although all his efforts to mount a Wells Coates exhibition had failed, there was still a small sum of money in the memorial fund. When I mentioned this to Ian Davis, Principal Lecturer in Architecture at Oxford Polytechnic, he immediately put forward the suggestion that an exhibition might be organised in Oxford. The outcome was the Wells Coates Exhibition Committee of architectural students and staff, and students on the Publishing Course, who run Oxford Polytechnic Press, have worked with them to produce this volume.

The exhibition, which opens at the Museum of Modern Art in Oxford in July 1979, has been planned as a travelling exhibition. It will go all over the United Kingdom and is expected to travel later to Canada and the United States. It contains twenty-one panels showing Wells's work. They are roughly chronological, but depart from strict date order where necessary so as to present subjects in an interesting and coherent way.

This book contains text and pictures on all Wells's major works included in the exhibition. The introductory section gives an overall perspective, with an emphasis on documents of the period and photographs of Wells at different ages. Section 2 goes straight to Yeoman's Row, his own flat, clearly revealing many of his ideals and methods in architecture and design. Thereafter the sections which depart from chronology are furniture (7), Ekco (8), 'design on display' (9), schemes for standardised housing (11), MARS and CIAM (19), and boat design (21). All these matters were the object of Wells's interest — in theory or in practice, successfully or not — over a span of time, and it is hoped that their presentation in this way will bring out the range of his achievement in different fields. A brief chronology lists all his major works together with biographical details.

Randal Bell, Wells's friend and client, has generously written a personal memoir of their activities together over the years. He adds a warmth to the portrait of Wells given elsewhere — a portrait necessarily restricted on the whole to his work.

Wells's words are quoted briefly here and there in the book and in the exhibition. To conclude the text it was decided to reprint one of his lectures, given in 1951 to the 'Present Question Conference'. Ever the idealist, he discusses the 'Freedom and Responsibility' of the architect, and somehow manages to bring in most of his favourite parables and quotations (Chinese philosophers being the favourite authors) while expounding his fundamental ideals in a post-war context. These ideals still seem worth restating and examining today.

Some people found my father difficult, and I suppose he was, for he was strong-minded, proud, quick to take offence, and too optimistic about his overdraft. I didn't find him difficult. He was serious, loving, and always eager to make me aware of the possibilities life had to offer. He liked to do things on a grand scale. He would recall his trip round the world at the age of seventeen, or a summer in his youth spent racing through the *whole* of Russian literature — or working all night at a congress. . . It was characteristic of him that he took his other interests seriously as well as architecture: cooking, sailing, motor cars, art. Even games could be treated seriously. 'Gamesmanship' was born at pre-war country house week-ends with Stephen Potter, Francis Meynell, Wells and others one-upping each other at tennis, backgammon, and the famous 'roof-game' (which consisted, as I remember it, of throwing a ball on to the roof and seeing what happened).

In his wartime letters to me (I was in Canada) Wells wrote enthusiastically about his sailing schemes.

Finally in 1948 his Wingsail Catamaran was successfully launched on the Norfolk Broads, and years later 'Fey Loong' sailed in the Solent. Although these designs were never marketed, I know that he got tremendous pleasure from all the work he put into both boats, and from sailing in them. I believe that in his architecture and design, the same thing was true: it was completely absorbing and rewarding, in spite of all the setbacks he suffered. Wells had numerous disappointments, but his life was not a disappointment. I hope that this volume will show what he did to create the 'new vision' in which he so passionately believed.

Laura Cohn
Oxford, May 1979

INTRODUCTION
by Sherban Cantacuzino*

The Modern Movement in architecture and design, itself a reaction to an extreme form of eclecticism, was essentially to do with principles and not with outward appearances, whatever today's revivalists may think. As Sir Leslie Martin has said, the important contribution of the 1920s and 1930s was the demonstration of a new attitude and a new method of work, rather than the creation of a set of forms to be adopted and manipulated. This new attitude, which involved a deep socio-political commitment, led to a thorough re-examination of human needs as related to architectural problems. The architects of the Modern Movement were concerned with the fundamental issues of planning and design rather than with the superficialities of style.

The great majority of Wells Coates's executed designs date from the 1930s, the era of the MARS Group and the rise of the English Modern Movement in which he played a leading part. It is one of the paradoxes of history that such a movement was able to thrive in an atmosphere of growing social and political disillusionment. On the one hand there was the brittle and irresponsible quality of the 1930s; on the other, the idealism of the architect pioneers. If Coates's life-style was necessarily affected by the long littleness of the 'thirties', it was always imbued with a seriousness — a passion — that made it remarkable. As much as any fellow-member of CIAM, he was dedicated to principles and to the single-minded search for ideal solutions.

Much of Coates's work in design and interiors has been destroyed. His two major architectural works, Lawn Road Flats and Palace Gate Flats, survive. When he began designing the Lawn Road project in 1929, English architecture was almost wholly eclectic and historicist. To achieve the final design solution took three years, and by that time the early works of the English Modern Movement had begun to appear in *The Architectural Review*: the buildings of Sir Owen Williams, Joseph Emberton, Connell and Ward, Howe and Lescaze, Tecton. Coates's early project for a pair of linked houses was soon abandoned, and the block of flats which was eventually built seems to this day a frank expression of functional needs and as original as any building of the Modern Movement. It demonstrates the application of the general principle of space that occupied all these architects.

Coates was living, and working for Tom Heron, in Welwyn Garden City when Jack Pritchard, who was in Paris working for Venesta Plywood, first approached him. Pritchard returned to London early in 1930, but Coates remained based in Welwyn until May the following year when he formed his small office in Bloomsbury. It was here that he and Jack and Molly Pritchard must have agreed the final brief for the Lawn Road Flats. Dated 19 May 1932, it proposed the erection of approximately twenty one-roomed flats on four floors. If possible one or more flats were to have two rooms and extra balcony space. The brief envisaged garage space for about eight cars and staff accommodation for a manageress. Much emphasis was laid on built-in storage fittings and central services including a small laundry and a kitchen.

The 'minimum flat', the show flat from Lawn Road, was exhibited by Pritchard's company Isokon at the Dorland Hall Exhibition in London in 1933. It was enthusiastically reviewed by *The Architectural Review* and had the desired effect of arousing sufficient interest in the form of deposits on flats to ensure building finance for the project. The block was completed the following summer.

The building has aesthetic shortcomings. Its technical shortcomings were, in a sense, more serious. They were due partly to the economies which the client was forced to impose as a result of the high tenders, and partly to the experimental nature of the construction. After the war extensive repairs were required to the roof, and to the concrete walls, and another major cause of deterioration was the metal windows, which corroded and stained the white

*The material for this essay has been drawn from the author's *Wells Coates: A Monograph* and from his essay 'Typology and Context', *The Architectural Review*, December 1977, with the addition of several statements from Laura Cohn.

façades. Later, modern architects learned from their mistakes and, like Wells Coates at Palace Gate, faced their concrete walls or used other materials.

For multi-storey buildings like Lawn Road Flats and Tecton's two Highpoint blocks, reinforced concrete was unquestionably the appropriate material with a respectable ancestry. Monolithic construction, though rarely used, enabled architects to give their buildings smooth uninterrupted wall planes without cheating, and consequently allowed the simple, cube-like forms which were regarded as part of the Modern Movement's aesthetic. But the greater flexibility of framed structure and the development, especially after the Second World War, of precast concrete and other sophisticated kinds of prefabricated panels, gradually rendered monolithic construction obsolete except where structural continuity remained the prime requirement.

Wells Coates's flats at 10 Palace Gate, completed in 1939, put into practice his ideas for 'planning in section'. The plan for the building is discussed, with illustration, in the pages of this volume devoted to Palace Gate. His 3-2 section was unquestionably superior to the 2-1 section which Tecton had used at Highpoint Two: the 2-1 section was easier to understand, but wasteful of space.

There is little doubt that, in a superficial way, the design of Palace Gate was influenced by Le Corbusier's Pavillon Suisse, completed in 1932 and certainly well known to Coates. The relationship of the two blocks, the curved wall and the use of artificial stone as a facing material to establish, as Coates said at the time, 'a module through the joints',[1] are all evidence of this influence. But the 3-2 section and its bold expression on the two main façades owed nothing to Le Corbusier and made an original contribution to modern architecture which was not to have the success it merited.

As Coates's first and only built essay in the genre, Palace Gate seems all the more remarkable. Underneath its dated skin, it retains extraordinary vitality and appropriateness. Much of the credit for getting Palace Gate built must go to Coates's client and developer, Randal Bell, who became the architect's counsellor and life-long friend. Bell writes of his experiences as client and friend in a separate essay in this volume.

Throughout his working life Wells Coates was involved in plans for mass-produced housing. As consultant to Isokon, his first commission was to design several house types which he called Isotype. The idea, a bold and original one, was to sell not houses, but parts of houses, and equipment standardised to fit. When this scheme failed Coates developed a design which, he said, 'is more directly related to the English customs and climate':[2] the Sunspan House.

Towards the end of the Second World War, Coates was seconded from the RAF to undertake consulting work for the Aircraft Industries Research Organisation on Housing (AIROH). His recommendation of the 'sectional unit' type of bungalow, which became the AIROH aluminium house, led to a Government order of 75,000 for continuous-line production. Later he prepared designs and a report on South American housing for the group of companies which had produced the original AIROH house.

At the same period, he was pursuing one of his most inventive ideas and one which also involved industrialised building and prefabrication. This was Room Units, described as 'Rooms in a Garden' and 'Rooms in a Frame'. Coates wrote enthusistically of the potential of Room Units for flats, hotels, and hostels, as well as for individual dwellings, but early unrealised schemes were followed by later disappointments and Room Units were never produced.

Wells Coates's understanding of the tool made him one of the best industrial designers of his time. His designs included wireless sets, electric fires, lighting fittings, handles, clocks, a piano, aeroplane interiors, furniture and fittings of all kinds, and boats.

His designs of wireless sets and electric fires for E.K. Cole show him at his most brilliant and technically integrated. The prize-winning AD 65 was followed by a number of other models, and after the war there were two particularly successful designs, the 'Radiotime' and the 'Princess-Handbag', the most distinguished of all. 'Thermovent' electric fires first appeared in 1937 and survived for some time after the war. Architects bought them and there is one in the Victoria and Albert Museum.

The furniture designed by Coates was simple in line, economical, and sometimes elegant, and included pieces for Isokon, Hilmor and PEL, and P.E. Gane. Then there were a good many special designs for private clients. Of a range of standard tubular steel furniture, first designed for Hilmor and PEL for the Embassy Court Flats, the simplest and most elegant was a day-bed.

Coates's interior work in the 1930s — which included shops, flats, a factory, and a nursery school — accorded with the modern architect's concept of 'total design'. The Strausses' flat at Kensington Palace Gardens was the most luxurious and complete conversion; the most numerous interior designs were the Cresta shops. He designed studios, furniture, and fittings for Broadcasting House ; a flat for Charles Laughton and Elsa Lanchester; a permanent stage set for the season at the Old Vic.

Throughout his life Coates expressed his ideas through the written word as well as through objects and buildings. As a boy in Japan (where he was born) he learned shorthand and typing, and his neatly typed diary of a journey to Kagoshima and Fukoka, in the spring of 1910, is evidence of his early proficiency. For the rest of his life Coates would think and write at the typewriter. He typed letters, reports, memoranda, specifications, manifestos, minutes, complaints, demands, visions. . .to do with his own work and with the groups of which he was a member: Unit One, MARS, and CIAM. In 1924 he got a job with the *Daily Express* and was sent to Paris; he returned to London after persuading Beverley Baxter, then editor, to have a science correspondent there. The short articles he published there cover an astonishing range and still make good reading.

After he had begun to practise successfully as an architect and designer, Coates wrote a number of articles which expressed his beliefs in general and his intentions and practice regarding particular jobs.

These include: 'Inspiration from Japan' and 'Materials for Architecture' (1931), 'Response to Tradition', 'Furniture Today — Furniture Tomorrow', and 'Modern Shops and Modern Materials' (1932); 'Planning in Section' (1937), 'The Conditions for an Architecture Today' (1938); and 'Freedom and Responsibility in the Experience of the Architect', a lecture given in 1951 and reprinted in the present book.

Ever since art became a revolutionary activity in the nineteenth century, painters and sculptors have formed groups so that they could more effectively put over their message. In 1933 Unit One was formed, a group of eleven consisting of seven painters, two sculptors, and two architects — Colin Lucas and Wells Coates. Unit One failed to outlive its second year; but the MARS Group, founded by Coates, survived, and made a vital contribution to architecture and planning, due in a very large measure to the energy and enthusiasm of Wells Coates. As a member of the MARS delegation to the famous fourth CIAM congress at Athens he met the international figures of modern architecture: Siegfried Giedion; J.L. Sert; Le Corbusier, who came to respect his work more than that of any other English architect; and Walter Gropius, who was soon to leave Nazi Germany for England and live in one of the Lawn Road Flats.

In his admirable memoir of Wells Coates, Sir James Richards wrote about MARS and CIAM: 'In the nineteen-thirties when the cause of modern architecture was being sustained by arguments and manifestos until such time as opportunities of building should come along, Wells was foremost in all the groups that did this necessary spadework — work which it is easy to disparage now when all we take note of in the *Charte d'Athène* is its sententious phraseology and its too rigid adherence to functional classifications. But such statements of dogma were landmarks in their time. It was their thorough working out of theoretical principles that made it possible to put theory into practice in due course. Today's architects take for granted freedoms and opportunities that would not be theirs if it had not been for the violent propagandists of the 'thirties.'[3]

The post-war period was one of little concrete achievement for Coates. It was one of intense and varied activity; but activity limited on the whole to the typewriter and the drawing board. Out of a number of large and exciting projects, including mass-produced low-cost housing, a hotel in Kent, a chain of cinemas in Scotland, a new town in Canada and the design of a mono-rail, only the Telekinema for the Festival of Britain went through to completion. Even his boat designs, which received wide acclaim, were financially unsuccessful.

Yet he lived life to the full: this did not mean that he was happy, but he worked, passionately, absorbed in realising his ideals. Writing enthusiastically about a development of the 3-2 system which he hoped to build all over Canada, Coates stated: 'Instead of designing a building to fit a given site, one designs a building to form the most economical unit of its own expression and purpose: and then to find a site in which, having

regard to variant town planning codes, the fully designed building may fit.'[4] There is no means of assessing Coates's performance because he never found any sites to build on. But the height, massing, sense of scale and choice of materials of the Palace Gate block, the only built example, show him to have been unexpectedly sensitive to his surroundings. Wells Coates's devotion to ideals did not impair his human feelings or his aesthetic sense.

Notes

1 Recalled from memory by Randal Bell.
2 Letter to Graham Maw, solicitor and chairman of Isokon, 7 February 1933.
3 Sir James Richards, *The Architectural Review*, December 1958.
4 Letter to Peter Thornton, an architect practising in Vancouver, 13 May 1958.

WELLS COATES

Wells Coates in uniform, France 1918

'. . . arrived Paris – St Lazare – on Monday 11th November at 8.30 – met by R.A.F. Capt. from H.Q. – to a Hotel for breakfast . . . The greatest day in the world – Germany signed the armistice this morning at 5 – and the last shot was fired . . . The Grand Boulevards are simply packed with mad singing cheering crowds . . . Everywhere we were greeted by cries of "Vive l'Angleterre" "Vive la Canada" – and surrounded on all sides.'

(Wells Coates, Diary, 11 November 1918)

Isometric drawing of Cresta Silks shop, Brompton Road, London 1929

'That 1929 Brompton Road shop made the most amazing use of the six letters C R E S T A in square format, and in very deep relief – I'd say they were two feet from back to front. While on the left-hand wall of the recess from pavement to plate-window the letters S I L K S projected so that they were legible only as you came along the pavement from the east: from straight in front, their form was totally abstract; very beautiful, very brilliant.'

(Patrick Heron, letter to Sherban Cantacuzino, 14 February 1973)

Dining room of 1 Kensington Palace Gardens after conversion 1932

'The lines of the chairs are so obviously comfortable that one is inclined to miss the important effect they have on the look of the room. The windows, covered with shantung silk, provide artificial light at night . . . Solid sound-proof sliding doors divide the two rooms.'

(Geoffrey Boumphrey, 'The Designers: 6. Wells Coates', Decoration Supplement to *The Architectural Review*, August 1932)

Broadcasting House: the gramophone turntable
bank in studio 6E, on the cover of *Radio Times*

'The Gramophone studies, the Dramatic Effects
studios, are as affirmative in form and intention
as is the spoken word of Mr. Wells Coates.'

(*The Listener*, 20 July 1932)

Lawn Road Flats kitchen 1934
Lawn Road Flats 1934

'In its planning and details and the ideas incorporated
it is one of the most significant buildings of this
epoch. It is scientifically designed for modern living
. . . One must congratulate Mr. Wells Coates on the
logic of his planning and the beauty of his smooth,
lean, elegant design.'

(*The Times*, 13 July 1934)

Unit One 1933

'Unit One may be said to stand for the expression
of a truly contemporary spirit, for that thing which
is recognized as peculiarly *of to-day* in painting,
sculpture, and architecture . . . The formation of
Unit One is a method of concentrating certain
individual forces; a hard defence, a compact wall
against the tide, behind which development can
proceed and experiment continue.'

(Paul Nash, letter to *The Times*, 12 June 1933)

Ekco AD 36 wireless set shown in advertisement 1934

'So far only a few, a mere handful, of plastic domestic articles have been successfully designed, and probably the best known is the Wells Coates radio receiving set of moulded Bakelite, a truly distinctive piece of work.'

('Plastics in the Home', *Decoration*, August 1936)

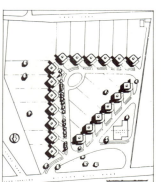

Brochure advertising Sunspan houses 1935

Site plan for 20 Sunspan houses at Thames Ditton, Surrey 1935

'Great interest was caused at the Ideal Home Exhibition at Olympia in 1934 by the "Sunspan" house erected there to the design of Wells Coates. This was a basic house unit of an ingenious plan form designed to be capable of a great number of variations . . .'

(*The Architectural Review*, December 1936)

Wells Coates sailing 1936

'There is nothing, absolutely nothing, to beat sailing.'

(Wells Coates, letter to his daughter, 29 July 1944)

Booklet on Embassy Court Flats showing balcony
1935
Sketch of sun decks at Embassy Court 1935

'Although it is in no way bizarre or freakish, it is
as modern as an aeroplane . . . It is the first building
in England to have both sun parlours and sun
balconies. In summer the sun parlours can be entirely
open to the air, while during windy weather the
special windows can be left partly open to act as
a screen to the wind. The flats on the ninth and
tenth floors are special sun terraces . . .'

(*Building*, August 1934)

'Embassy Court . . . appears as one of the more
refined elements amid the present hurly-burly of the
seafront — except, of course, the Regency terraces
. . . the aesthetic was rather in advance of the building
technology with the result that a lot of fabric,
services and fittings have had to be renewed . . . "Steel,
concrete and glass" was the cri de coeur, but these
materials need correct detailing and protection if
they are to withstand the particular kind of
atmospheric pollution caused by salt-laden spray
which blows in gusts off the sea, the buffeting winds
and lashing coastal rains.'

('Embassy Court Revisited', *Building Design*,
14 March 1975)

Wells Coates at Tufton Manor, Hampshire 1937

'About 1935 this house in Hampshire became the
regular scene of week-end house parties . . . By car
to Tufton came Walter Goetz, then the cartoonist
of the Daily Express, and his wife Jill; Margaret and
Ashley Havinden, the Duncan Millers and Paul
Reilly . . . Regular guests were Mary and Stephen
Potter, and James Thurber.'

(Sherban Cantacuzino, *Wells Coates: A Monograph*,
Gordon Fraser, 1978, p.30)

Wells Coates photographed by Howard Coster 1937

'Wells Coates, founder of the Mars (Modern Architectural Research) group, originator of the flatlet, designer of public utility buildings, such as broadcasting studios, laboratories, consulting-rooms, and one of the most practical members of the slum clearance movement, always meant to be a constructor. But circumstances, wanderlust, and the war prevented his start until he was thirty-five.'

(*The Bystander*, 3 November 1937)

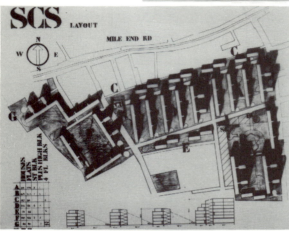

Slum Clearance Scheme, Stepney 1937

'Beaumont Estate in Stepney was a group of 750 houses — without a bathroom amongst them . . . On this Wells produced drawings for a redevelopment scheme . . . With his usual brilliance when faced with a challenge, he sited the first buildings in the street so that no one was displaced until there was a new home to go to.'

(Randal Bell, essay on Wells Coates in the present volume)

Palace Gate Flats from the south 1939

'In his work Wells Coates is quite clearly the sensitive engineer . . . Of the many variations of a design which will achieve its purpose as completely as may be, he chooses that one which looks best. His preliminary analysis of the conditions is singularly complete and acute; his solution is often refreshingly original: he adds nothing for effect — and he gives us from time to time veritable glimpses of what I have called the New Beauty.'

(Geoffrey Boumphrey, 'The Designers: 6. Wells Coates', Decoration Supplement to *The Architectural Review*, August 1932)

Wells Coates sailing with Randal Bell 1937

'We sailed and fished at Shaldon in Devon and designed sails for my 16 footer.'

(Randal Bell, essay on Wells Coates in the present volume)

Invitation to CIAM 5 Congress 1937

'CIAM will help you to be a citizen and an individual. It will put you in touch with the infinite cosmos and with the common forms of nature — with God and with the spirits of the earth. It will provide you with places and buildings where you can live a full life, both in mind and body so that you will no longer be crushed, but can rise up and shine.'

(Le Corbusier, in *The Heart of the City*, ed. J. Tyrwhitt et al, Lund Humphries, 1952, p. xii)

MARS Exhibition poster 1938

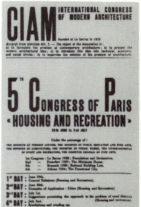

'The MARS group represents a violent reaction against impressive architecture . . . To the classical Baalbekian list of building materials, stone and bricks and mortar, it adds concrete with a steel skeleton, glass, and steel without any concrete. I must not say that in using these materials for utilitarian ends it is indifferent to the aspect of the result. Indeed, artistic instinct is at the very root of the matter even if the more fanatical Martians do produce buildings that are staggeringly unlike Adelphi Terrace and Fitzroy Square. No matter: we shall have to get used to them, even if the only way to escape from their unusualness is to get inside them . . .'

(George Bernard Shaw, Preface to Exhibition Catalogue)

Cover of Ideal Home magazine with The Homewood, Esher, Patrick Gwynne in association with Wells Coates 1939

'One of the most agreeable examples of modern domestic architecture in England.'

(Sherban Cantacuzino, *Wells Coates*, p. 87)

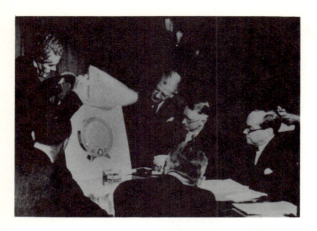

Wells Coates showing a new radio cabinet to engineers at E.K. Cole 1945

'Perhaps the nicest tribute to Coates's industrial designs was paid by Mr Burtenshaw, the chief draughtsman of Ekco, when he said quite simply that all Wells Coates's designs had been practicable propositions.'

(Sherban Cantacuzino, *Wells Coates*, p. 27)

Model of the Wingsail Catamaran, shown at Britain Can Make It Exhibition 1946

'At the same time, I have designed (or invented) a new type of sail-gear and sail-cloth for my ship, for which two people (in two different industries concerned) have expressed interest. This is an entirely new form of sail, highly experimental of course, but based on elementary knowledge of aerodynamics, from the observations of birds' wings and from aircraft experience . . .'

(Wells Coates, letter to his daughter, 11 February 1945)

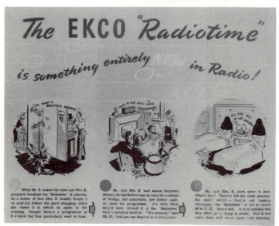

Leaflet for Ekco Radiotime 1946

'What is the EKCO "Radiotime"? (1) IT'S A RADIO SET (2) AN ELECTRIC CLOCK (3) AN ALARM-CLOCK (4) IT SWITCHES ITSELF ON (5) IT SWITCHES ITSELF OFF Few of us actually *like* getting up in the morning . . . We believe it is much nicer to wake up to the gentle but persistent tones of an orchestra than to be "hit on the head" by the strident clatter of an alarmbell.
EKCO "RADIOTIME" MODERN AS THE HOUR'

(Centre panel of leaflet, E.K. Cole Ltd, Southend-on-Sea)

Wells Coates with Le Corbusier at CIAM 6 Congress, Bridgwater 1947

'One remembers him most warmly at those international meetings in which he delighted to take part, especially the periodic congresses of CIAM . . . He could take his place unselfconsciously alongside the internationally known figure who presided at these congresses. . . and his gaiety on these occasions was unforced as, in the hot summer sunshine, shirt-sleeved but immaculate, he busied himself with meeting after meeting. . .'

(Sir James Richards, *The Architectural Review*, December 1958, pp.357-60)

Wells Coates after return to Canada 1957
Drawing for Mass Rapid Transit report 1957
Wells Coates on the running board of his Lancia Lambda 1951

'The fact is that in spite of all attempts to get things going since my return to practice, some of my principal objectives seem to be blocked, both in the architectural and in the industrial design fields, and the recent stoppages of certain works, coupled with the statement of policy regarding capital appropriations, delineate a very weak picture for the future for chaps like myself . . .'

(Wells Coates to George Strauss, 3 November 1947)

'His long addiction to Lancias (the splendid specimen shown above combines a 1925 chassis with a 1928 engine) is perhaps due to their architectural quality.'

(*Vogue*, April 1951)

'It doesn't really matter in the long run that there are so few Wells Coates buildings for posterity to remember him by, because *all* the modern buildings we see when we look around us are collectively his memorial.'

(Sir James Richards, *The Architectural Review*, December 1958, pp. 357-60)

18 YEOMAN'S ROW 1935

'That is the choice, the use of the new resources of materials as the prisoners — the slaves — of old habits, old social prejudices, old *visual* prejudices; or as the means of new forms, new habits of life, a new vision. The time has arrived for architects to reflect and to create.' [1]

'New habits of life, a new vision'. In the redesigning of his own studio flat on the upper floor of a London terraced house, Coates created the 'machine for living in' by making ingenious use of a 2-1 section. In this he lived from 1935 until 1955 with the exception of the war years. Most of the space was kept open as living areas, but the rear quarter was divided horizontally to provide two 'bed cabins'. In Coates's words: 'You cannot get two complete floor levels, with proper headroom, in a total floor to ceiling height of 12 ft. Your programme demands that the largest possible space of full ceiling is available for "living" in. You do not want a "separate" bedroom...The normal "void" under a bed is captured to provide head room in the bathroom or the kitchen, where you want it...' [2]

To preserve the appearance from the street the huge studio window was retained, but fitted with obscured glass. To improve the sound and heat insulation he added an inner skin of sliding plate glass, which gave access to a plant trough between the inner and outer glazing.

The influence on Coates of his years in Japan is clearly reflected in the interior design. He believed that furniture should be 'built-in' wherever possible: 'Your furniture and equipment is to be an integral part of the design, planned to enclose every cubic inch of space, and disposed to use at every point.' [3] This belief was demonstrated in his studio by the use of built-in bookcases, drinks cupboard, bed 'spaces', radio, and desk, which although free-standing 'telescoped' into the bookcase to form a buffet table top for parties. 'I do not like big sofas and easy chairs', he wrote, 'so I make a hearth scene, *a la japonais*': [4] enormous cushions rested on Japanese matting, stretched over one inch of cushion rubber. Coates commented that 'your book, your glass, your cigarette are at hand at the proper level and cannot be carelessly knocked over'. [5]

Coates's daughter writes: 'I lived in the flat for twelve years after 1947. The height of the room, and the effects of the ladders and the two levels, were perhaps the most striking things about the studio. It was airy, spacious, cool; it was unlike anywhere else. Even in 1962, it seemed more modern than anything else I knew. It actually affected the way one thought and lived.'

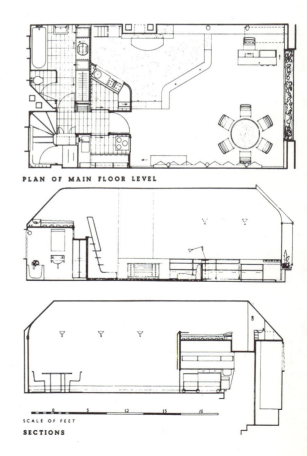

PLAN OF MAIN FLOOR LEVEL

SCALE OF FEET

SECTIONS

Living area viewed from main bed cabin

3 Integrated design

CRESTA SILKS

Alec Walker and Tom Heron were partners in a small silks-dying factory in St. Ives. In the summer of 1928 Coates met Alec Walker, and was appointed to work on standardising shop-fittings in plywood. Shortly afterwards Heron and Walker dissolved the partnership. Tom Heron left to found Cresta Silks Ltd, and in June 1929 Coates was asked to design the interior of the Cresta factory in Welwyn Garden City.

Planned within a standard rectangular shell, the factory included a model salon and a large mirrored fitting room. All the doors and built-in wardrobes were fitted with Coates's characteristic D-handles, purpose designed, as were the radiators, furniture and fittings.

Tom Heron's Cresta Silks set out to achieve in a three-year programme a unified manufacturer-to-consumer system. Towards this end Coates was

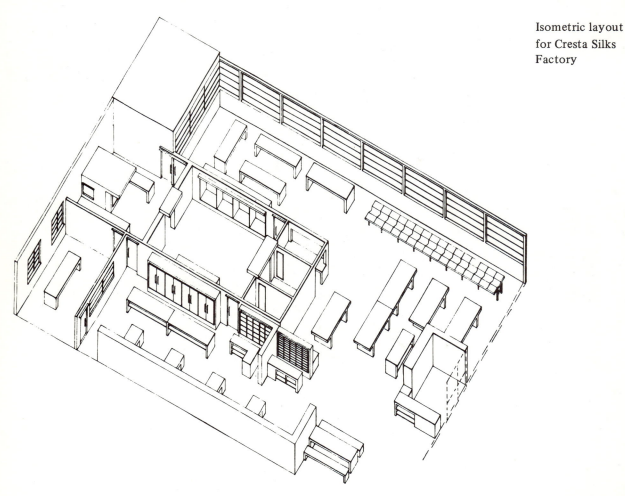

Isometric layout
for Cresta Silks
Factory

asked to design an inexpensive standardised shop which would make it economically possible to rent short-term leases on prestigious and important thoroughfares. The success of Coates's pioneering work inspired many companies to open outlets in new districts without the large financial outlays normally involved.

The first shop in Brompton Road, London, was designed shortly after the factory was finished. It became famous for the letters C R E S T A, designed within a square format and proportioned to have maximum effect when viewed from across the street. The letters were constructed in metal and supported by the canopy which was framed in deal and faced with ¼″ double sided galvanised steel plywood. The back screen of the display window with its two access panels was framed in steel sections and glazed to provide daylight illumination for the interior. The glass used was Georgian wired rough cast, sand-blasted on one side. The soffit and sides to the display window were of ½″ batten board and the

base was faced with ¼″ copper plymax which was illuminated by concealed lighting in the soffit. The paving stones fronting the shop were of pink terrazzo. The total cost, which included services and finishes, was £983.00; £17.00 within the budget figure set for the scheme.

Coates went on to design Cresta Shops in Baker Street and Bond Street, London, and in Bournemouth, Bromley and Brighton, the principal materials used throughout being plywood, glass, and framing of standard steel sections.

At the time of the completion of the Brompton Road shop Coates received praise for his 'revolutionary concept'.[1] When asked his motives for this particular style he replied that it was to show that the 'accepted habit. . .to use certain expensive materials in the construction of shop fronts, in order to convey a luxury effect'[2] was unnecessary. 'The first essential aim in building a shop front', he said, 'is to give it a form which is at once restful and quiet.'[3]

Cresta Silks,
Bournemouth 1929

BBC STUDIOS, LONDON 1932

'Broadcasting had grown enormously during the
nine years at the Savoy Hill Studio. Studio
accommodation had grown too, but not nearly fast
enough. . . Artists had to work in conditions that
took more out of them than the work itself
demands.'[1] In 1928, when the BBC were informed
of the available site on the corner of Portland Place
and Langham Street, they commissioned Lt Col
G. Val Myer to design and build new premises suitable
for their rapidly increasing activities. Raymond
McGrath was appointed as Decorations Consultant
in association with Wells Coates and Serge
Chermayeff, who were to design the interiors.

Each designer worked closely with BBC engineers
to acoustically determined requirements; using
materials especially designed for purposes of
absorption, resonance or reverberation.

Coates's share of the design was singled out by
one critic of the time 'as perhaps the most significant
of all'.[2] He was responsible for the design of the
news studios 4A and 4B, the main effects studio 6D,
two gramophone studios 6E and 7E, an experimental
effects studio 7D and two dramatic controls rooms.

The news studios, separated by the news editors
lobby, were used for news reading and small
gramophone recitals. The main effects studio, which
occupied a depth of two floors, included a revolving
table on which were laid various surfaces, such as
felt, rubber and wood, for use in the creation of
sound effects. Other effects — slamming, latching,
locking and sliding, could be obtained from a special
door; anchor and rowing effects from a water tank,
and thunder from a large sheet of steel suspended
from the ceiling. The floor was divided into three
areas: one carpeted, another in plain cement and
another in wood. Suspended from the ceiling was
a doubly counter-balanced microphone, which was
ingeniously designed by Coates to free the floor of
stands and cables. The two gramophone studios,
which stood one above the other overlooking the
main effects studio, were equipped with a bank of
six turntables controlled from a central 'mixer
unit'. The two dramatic controls rooms were used
during the production of a single play. Each room
was equipped with a loudspeaker, for monitoring
progress of the production; telephones, for
communicating to the main control rooms; and a
centrally placed control unit capable of linking eleven
studios and possessed of microphones for issuing
instructions to artists, cue light cut out and volume
controls. The unit itself was framed in tubular steel
sections supported and fixed to the floor at one end

The double-height dramatic effects studio

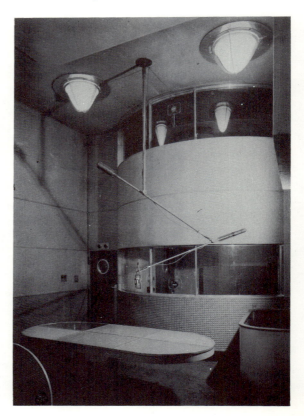

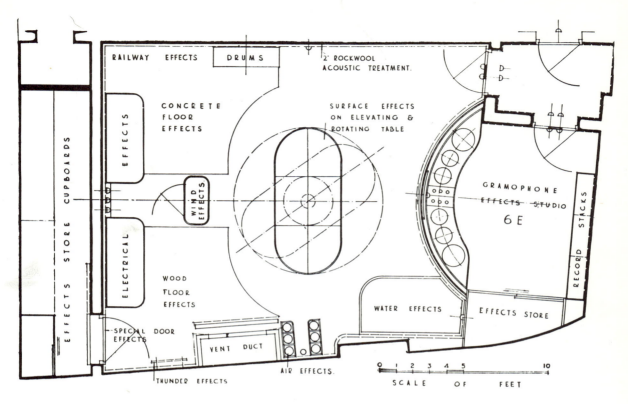

Plan of double-height dramatic effects studio

by two free-standing legs, at the other end by enclosed legs forming an accessible duct through which wires and cables rose from beneath the floor.

Sherban Cantacuzino writes: 'Inevitably, the studios could not survive the changing requirements of broadcasting technique, but their realisation at that moment had repercussions of a wider nature for which architects and designers were to be grateful.'[3]

1 KENSINGTON PALACE GARDENS 1932

Wells Coates's largest commission as an interior designer was for Mr and Mrs George Strauss. He was asked to strip the elaborate Victorian interior of their house and design it afresh. 'The past is not always behind us, but more often in front blocking the way' was a favourite saying. Here was the golden opportunity to sweep the past away.

In the entrance hall Coates replaced 'a large oval mirror in carved and gilt foliated frame, a pair of Koodoo horns with skull and shield and a pair of Moorish chairs inlaid with ivory'[1] with a circular mirror in a wood surround cellulosed 'pale copper', a copper-plated frame table with a rough cast glass top, and a screen of chinese red laquer and pale green glazing.

In the drawing room he removed the decorative Venetian glass candelabrum, stripped the walls and fireplace and converted it into a mirrored ballroom illuminated in a variety of intensities by a series of lighting troughs. The room was decorated by a low wall frieze of ballet figures painted by John Armstrong.

In the dining room a dining table of laminated wood veneered in English burr walnut supported on a steel frame and a set of high back upholstered chairs took the place of the richly carved table and chairs and massive carved oak sideboard 'with lofty back, fitted with cupboards and shelves'.[2] The steel legs of the dining table were fixed to the floor and encased in pale green rough cast glass, the upper parts of which were illuminated from the underside.

In the principal bedroom the double bed, with the headboard inclined at an angle of 75°, was recessed between the two banks of built-in wardrobes. On either side of the bed the lower sections of the wardrobes contained double trays hidden behind spring doors. When operated from the bed the spring door opened and the tray slid out to form a breakfast table.

'Our society is above all determined to be free',[3] wrote Coates, and he believed that modern man could become freer by ridding himself of unnecessary belongings. His scheme should be seen not only as functional but as a truly modern design — in the words of Geoffrey Boumphrey: 'The quality which seems to me to mark Mr Wells Coates so strongly among his contemporaries is his clear perception of the tendencies of modern life. Among the cross-currents of habit and purpose he perceives the move of the tide — the resultant of its singularly intractable components. In the field of interior equipment (if we leave beauty out of it for the moment) he would, I think, rank mobility close after convenience. He sees modern living as essentially dynamic...'[4]

The new dressing-table, with double-backed revolving mirrors each having a slightly different tint

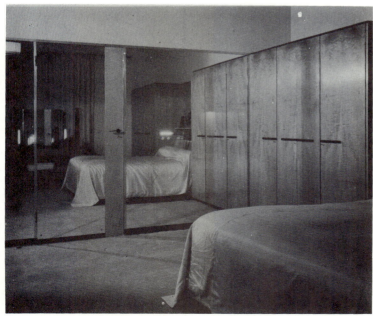

The main bedroom before
and after conversion

Wells Coates believed that furnishings — like heating, lighting, and sanitation — should be integrated into architecture: 'instead of being added on to the completed building' they 'are, or ought to be, integral with it, a part of its construction, and therefore of its form'.[1] The interior designer and the architect draw on the same functional inspiration: 'Modern design must begin from the interior plan (including furniture and equipment) as generator, and make explicit externally the processes, functions and qualities included in the whole scene.'[2] This was the ethic of the Bauhaus, whose principles and practice so strongly influenced the development of industrial design. Coates designed bookcases for the Isokon partnership, formed in 1931, of which Jack Pritchard writes: 'When we formed Isokon, our plan was to set up a financially viable business in England which would provide a focus for the new ideas and techniques largely inspired by the Bauhaus.'[3] Walter Gropius and Marcel Breuer also joined Isokon after their arrival in England.

Coates's designs can be seen both in mass-produced furniture and fittings and in his individual pieces for private clients in their flats, shops, and houses. The first production designs were for the Cresta factory and shops (1929-32). The bookcase units for Isokon (1932) were shown in the Dorland Hall Exhibition of the minimum flat and used in Lawn Road Flats. In the mid 1930s Coates began designing tubular steel furniture for Hilmor and PEL, which included a tubular steel day bed, a desk, and lightweight canvas covered chairs, all used in the newly completed Embassy Court Flats. For P.E. Gane of Bristol he designed a whole range of wooden furniture, which included fitted cupboards, shelves and a three-legged table (1936).

Perhaps the least recognised yet most used design by Coates are his D-handles or 'Tayloroid bow handles', manufactured from 1928 by Taylor, Pearce and Co in aluminium and finished in a synthetic resin. Fixing was from behind with a screw into a steel plug filling at the end of the tube handle. Designed principally for built-in furniture, they were also used on swing doors, making the use of finger plates unnecessary.

The one-off designs were produced for his interiors for various clients; among them were his own flat at Yeoman's Row, the conversion of 1 Kensington Palace Gardens for Mr and Mrs George Strauss, the penthouse flat of Mr and Mrs Hans Juda at 10 Palace Gate, the flat at 34 Gordon Square for Charles Laughton and Elsa Lanchester, and the penthouse flat for Jack and Molly Pritchard at No 32 Lawn Road Flats.

Radiators, lighting fittings and clocks were also included in many of his interiors; two clocks, the 'Queen's Clock' and the 'King's Clock' were specially designed for the Festival of Britain in 1951. His designs break down the divisions between 'furniture', 'fittings' and 'architecture': all are part of the total design.

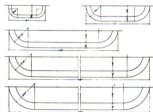

D-handles

T R A D E   N O T E S

[BY F. R. S. YORKE, A.R.I.B.A.]

Door Handles

THE bow handles designed some years ago by Mr. Wells Coates, and used by him on his own work, are now being manufactured for general sale by Taylor, Pearse & Co., from tubes made by Tube Products, Ltd. They are finished in Tayleroid, a synthetic resin that retains its polish and will not chip or crack.

The design is the result of an attempt to provide a convenient handle for swing doors and doors fitted with a ball catch. The bow handles may be fixed either vertically or horizontally. Their length and spacing from the door face enable finger-plates to be eliminated, as they obviously accommodate people of different heights.

The smallest handle is 4 in. long giving ample room for all fingers, and affording a comfortable grip.

Where used for drawers, these handles have the advantage of giving a more distributed pull along the drawer front than is afforded by the normal type, so minimizing the "binding" that occurs when the drawer is pulled asymmetrically.

The fixing is by means of a Whitworth

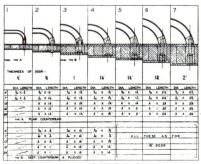

Details of door handles designed by Wells Coates. See note on this page.

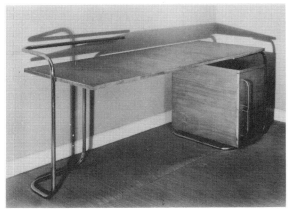

Tubular steel desk (Hilmor and PEL)

Tubular steel day bed (Hilmor and PEL)

Tubular steel and canvas covered chairs (Hilmor and PEL)

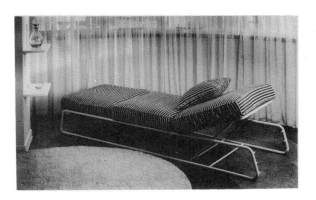

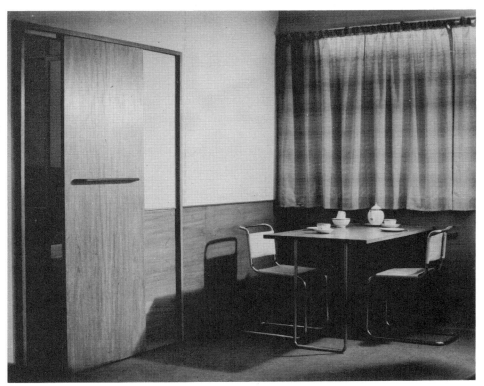

DESIGNS FOR EKCO

In 1934 Coates wrote: 'A radio set should never be disguised as something else. It has its own important function in the home and is in many cases a possession regarded more as the indoor equivalent of a car than a piece of furniture.'[1]

In 1930 W. Verrello and Eric Cole, managing directors of Ekco, built a large moulding plant for plastics in Southend. Owing to the high cost of tooling, plastic manufacturers could not speculate with ill-considered designs. To ensure the best in design for their products Ekco instigated a competition for wireless cabinets. Entries were submitted from many top designers, including Serge Chermayeff, Raymond McGrath, Jesse Collins and Misha Black. Coates won in 1932 with the only circular wireless, a shape which was praised for showing a complete understanding of the functional aspects of wirelesses. The shape, built around the circular loudspeaker, exploited the moulding process of bakelite. The absence of sharp corners reduced the number of moulding tools required, and therefore lowered costs.

The significance of Coates's design may not be easily realised today. In the early thirties a great many patents were still being taken out for moulded plastic imitations of other materials. In reaction to this the periodical *Decoration* wrote: 'Plastics are brand new materials with certain very special characteristics, and in order to utilise them to full and lasting advantage they must be moulded into shapes which will prove convenient, practical, and yet be good looking, and so adapted that the material itself is exploited to full advantage. A new tradition must be created from plastics, and it is doing these materials an ill service by adopting make-shift styles . . . What is most urgently needed is professional designers with a working knowledge of plastics who can be trusted to evolve a distinctly new and satisfying Plastic Style.'[2]

Ekco saw Coates's design as a 'practical proposition' satisfying the requirement for a 'Plastic Style', and after its appearance in 1934 the AD 65 wireless became one of the most popular sets in Britain.

Coates's wireless designs for Ekco included the AD 36 in 1934, which sold at 8½ guineas in a walnut or black finish, the cheapest in the range. In 1935 came the AC 76 which was a larger model with better performance. It was mounted on a wooden stand and finished in plain bakelite and chrome. After the war, Coates designed in 1946 a combined wireless and alarm, the 'Radiotime', which was finished in 'ivory' plastic with a cross-hatched copper fascia. Two years later he completed his range with the 'Princess-Handbag' portable wireless.

In 1937 Wells Coates designed the first floor-standing range of electrical fires for Ekco. These 'Thermovent' heaters were available in 1 or 2 kilowatt models, housed in black or brown phenolic plastic cases, and remained in production for sixteen years.

The PC 1 Thermovent electric fire 1937

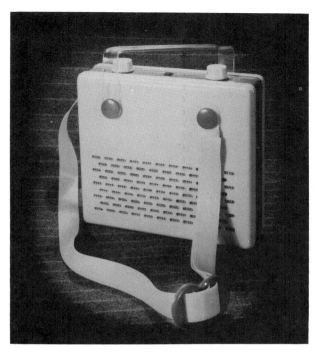

The A 22 wireless 1946

The AD 65 wireless 1934

'The elegant "Princess" portable — lightweight all day. Virtually unbreakable. . . A wonderful set for outdoor use — you can take it anywhere'

The Radiotime 1946

VENESTA STAND 1931

In 1931 Venesta Plywoods Ltd sponsored a
competition to design a stand for the British Empire
Trade Exhibition in Manchester. There were 115
entries, among them C.F.A. Voysey, Serge Chermayeff
and Maxwell Fry. Coates's winning design incorporated
as many practical uses of Venesta products as possible,
and provided space in which the public could view
the exhibits and consult salesmen. Samples of plywood
and plymax were displayed mounted on rotating
panels on the rear dividing screen.

The assessors commented: 'His plan is remarkably
good, ensuring a circulation, allowing samples to be
seen and handled, while the office accommodation
is well arranged. . .it definitely invites the visitor
onto the stand'. They concluded that 'the advantages
of employing a competent designer should be brought
home to manufacturers'.[1] The stand was the first of
a series produced for Venesta from 1931 to 1935.

TELEKINEMA 1951

Like most of the buildings in the Festival of Britain,
the Telekinema was a temporary structure. It was
designed to show the public the latest in television
and film projection, and provided a testing ground
for modern equipment. To accommodate 400 people
on the small site Coates and his assistant Peter Bender
made use of 'sectional planning' on a parallel plan.
Coates explained: 'We arrived at what might be called
a "lobster claw" section: with the upper claw reaching
into the balcony, the lower to the back row of the
stalls: the projection room and its equipment being
the tidy morsel tightly gripped in these.'[3]

Acknowledging the experimental nature of the
building, Coates glazed the back wall to the projecting
room to give the public a view of the 'working parts'
and enable the television cameras to televise scenes
in the foyer. The site, within fifteen feet of
Hungerford Bridge, created a particular acoustic
problem. To solve it Coates specified 10" thick
reinforced concrete walls lined with sound-absorbing
surfaces.

OLD VIC SET 1933

In 1933 Wells Coates designed a permanent stage for
a season of plays at the Old Vic Theatre, Waterloo
Road, London. The set comprised a variety of levels
and a useful number of exits which formed 'an
ingenious and generally efficient solution of problems
essentially vital to the producer'.[2] Construction was
mainly of plywood and canvas.

The auditorium and projection room of the
Telekinema

The Venesta stand 1931

Players on the stage at the Old Vic

HAMPDEN NURSERY SCHOOL 1936

The Hampden Nursey School in London occupied the ground floor rooms of a large Victorian house at 14 Holland Park. This scheme was initiated by Mr and Mrs George Strauss, and Coates and his assistant Denys Lasdun were employed to design a space that would allow the children to express their natural feelings and abilities. The school illustrates two important aspects of the 1930s. First was the concept of 'total design', in which a room was planned on the basis of function, every item being designed or specially selected to serve as a part of a strongly unified scheme. Secondly, the design reflected the interest and enthusiasm of progressive people in the 1930s for nursery school education.

Coates created a large sliding-folding window, to let in the fresh air and sunshine: a symbolic gesture, as the original sash window would have been adequate. Inside, the perimeter walls were lined with built-in cupboards, in which were stored the newly designed 'educational toys'. In the front room he incorporated a large blackboard, and a mezzanine with a retractable slide. In the back room was a sand pit and a climbing frame.

The front room

NEWS CHRONICLE SCHOOLS COMPETITION 1937

A year later Wells Coates and Denys Lasdun began
work on what is quoted as being one of the most
exciting architectural events of the decade, the News
Chronicle Schools Competition. The aim of the
competition was to improve the design of elementary
schools by taking advantage of modern building
techniques and rational design. The competition
was divided into two sections: the first was to be
a design for a school in an urban district for 480
children, and the second was for a school for 160
children in a rural district; both were to be for mixed
senior schools. Many leading architects were amongst
the 250 entries, out of which 38 reached the second
stage. Wells Coates entered for the first section, for
which he was highly commended and was placed
fourth.

    R. Gardner-Medwin, in reviewing the competition,
said that it was necessary 'to tackle and eliminate
one by one the noise, smell, dinginess, cramped
circulation and echoing quadrangles which are the
faults of contemporary schools'.[1] Coates's design,
set on a spacious urban site, certainly fitted Gardner-
Medwin's criteria. On the ground floor a series of
classroom wings opened off a central spine consisting
of changing facilities, practical rooms, and a covered
playground. Coates raised the staff accommodation
on stilts in order to retain the ground floor as part
of the open space, where trees, gardens and an
outdoor theatre were an integral part of the design.

    Significantly the assessors commented that the
layout had been conceived from the child's point of
view, and praised the absence of any institutional
flavour. The ideas expressed during the competition
were to be developed further in the 1944 Education
Act and subsequent school building.

Block plan showing the carefully considered garden
and planting layout

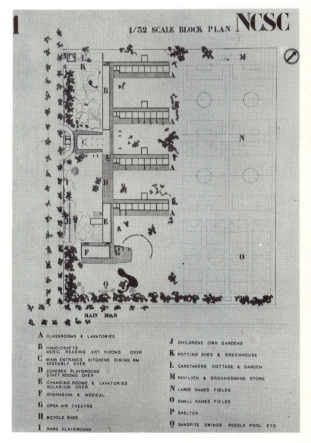

ISOTYPES 1931

In 1930 Wells Coates became consultant architect to Jack Pritchard's company Isokon, and was asked to design four types of house. The first of these materialised in 1931 as the Isotype Dwelling of the SA (single storey) or DA (double storey) type. Coates wrote to Isokon: 'The external shell will be made up of a certain number of units whose dimensions have been carefully worked out to give the maximum space for the minimum cost, while at the same time giving the maximum interchangeability.'[1]

Coates's idea was to sell standardised unit parts of houses, fully equipped, but the experimental nature of the design failed to satisfy the authorities. So Isokon decided to find a suitable site and build an Isotype Dwelling as an experiment. When the project proved to have too many practical problems, Coates proposed a new scheme, Sunspan, which he took to the builders E.L. Berg.

SUNSPAN 1934

Designed by Wells Coates and David Pleydell-Bouverie, the first Sunspan House, a two-storey version, was shown in 1934 at the Daily Mail Ideal Home Exhibition at Olympia. It was the only house exhibited that was fully furnished and equipped to the architect's specification, which raised considerable interest. Morton Shand wrote in *The Architects' Journal*: 'Perhaps the first serious English contribution to domestic planning forms since that famous discovery of the "free", open planning of the English country house took the continent by storm at the beginning of the century'.[2]

The plan, intended to have some degree of flexibility, was within a square with the corners orientated towards the points of the compass. So

Plans and elevations of Isotype Dwelling, DA type

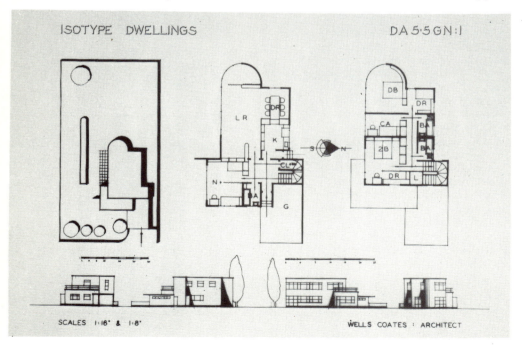

ISOTYPE DWELLINGS   DA 5·5 GN:1

SCALES 1:16" & 1:8"   WELLS COATES : ARCHITECT

SCALE 1 INCH = 8 FEET   SUNSPAN PLANS AND DESIGNS ARE THE EXCLUSIVE PROPERTY AND COPYRIGHT OF THE ARCHITECTS   WELLS COATES & PLEYDELL-BOUVERIE ARCHITECTS 15 ELIZABETH ST. S.W.1.

Plans, sections and elevations of the Sunspan House,
Daily Mail Ideal Home Exhibition, 1934

instead of a south front there were south-east and south-west walls, which meant that sun could enter the living room all day long, while the kitchen, bathroom and maid's room had north-east or north-west aspects. The dining room and study to right and left of the living room were separated off by sliding partitions which could be opened to provide a fan-shaped room 38′ across. Above the living room was the principal bedroom; both were fitted with sliding

windows rounding off the southern apex.

Coates planned several varieties of Sunspan, from a five-bedroomed house to a small week-end cottage, all made possible by prefabricated production. Floors, walls and roof were made of Lewis dovetailed steel sheeting fixed to both sides of a steel frame and plaster finished. Some eighteen houses were built in all, but most did not follow the architect's specification.

37

ROOM UNITS 1946-47

'Room Unit Production. . .has been designed to meet the flexible needs of human beings for shelter, for planned and serviced equipment, and for that select value of a personal environment — the aesthetic choice — which is an individual and family right.'[3]

The ideas which began before the war and were developed through Coates's work on the 'emergency housing' programme in 1944 and the designs for the AIROH House finally reached fruition in 1947 with Room Units. These were designed as a solution to the varied demands of living accommodation through the exploitation of factory standardisation. Two types were to be mass produced, 'Rooms in a Garden, where the units are used in a garden setting in various layouts, and Rooms in a Frame, where the units are linked in special ways to a prepared structural frame-

work'.[4] Coates proposed that the construction should be of 'insulated structural laminates', which could be made in one of four ways: a laminate of paper or fabric; a cast light alloy; a cast steel reinforced concrete; or welded aluminium.

The basic Room Unit was divided by a 'vertical spine member' (located to take the handling strains) 'to give a 7′ 6″ square floor area to the Equipment or Service Room, leaving a dimension of 12′ 6″ x 7′ 6″ for the Main Room floor'.[5]

Basic components and production assembly sequence of Room Units: Rooms in a Garden

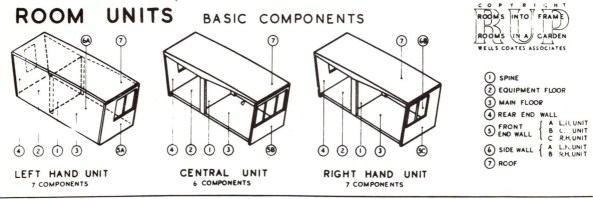

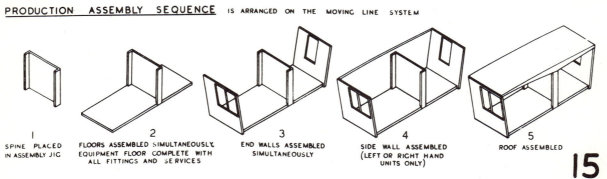

38

Rooms in a Garden

Coates suggested that a person who possessed only one of the said units could have his house lowered by gantry to a lorry, transported to the country and slid into a vacant frame for week-ends.

LAWN ROAD FLATS

Lawn Road Flats, Wells Coates's best-known building, has a long history of development. Jack Pritchard had bought an inexpensive site on the fringe of Hampstead to build himself a house. While the project was still in the early design stages he became aware of the work of Wells Coates and asked him to take over the design. Coates did so but pointed out that one 'ought not' to build a house on a London site, one 'ought' to build flats, an imperative that Pritchard understood. Molly Pritchard prepared a brief, which included an instruction that the building must not be out of date by 1950. It took three years to prepare the final brief and in May 1932 the plan was agreed.

The building seen from the south-east

The minimum flat

Although not involved in the 1929 CIAM conference in Frankfurt, which was actively devoted to minimum space, Coates was inspired by its conclusions and on 11 September 1930 he wrote in a memorandum to Jack Pritchard about 'the paramount importance of building in largish units, as the building of small attached houses will very quickly be discarded, when it is shown how economical and comfortable and convenient other methods may be.'[1] The 'other methods' referred to were to lead to his development of the 'minimum flat' for Lawn Road: his answer to the search of the Modern Movement for the 'minimum' or 'ration' dwelling.

'Lawn Road flats', wrote *The Times*, 'have been designed with special reference to the circumstances of the bachelor or young married professional or business person.'[2] They were admirably suited to those without possessions, such as the newly arriving artists and architects escaping Nazi Germany. The list of early tenants included Walter Gropius, Marcel Breuer, Arthur Korn and Moholy-Nagy, as well as Agatha Christie and Lance Sieveking.

The five-storey building when it was opened in 1934 consisted of twenty-two flats of the 'minimum type' which had a main bed-sitting room, a dressing room linked to a bathroom, and a kitchenette. In addition there were four south-facing two-roomed flats divided by sliding panels, three studio flats with large north-facing windows, and one large penthouse on the fifth floor for the Pritchards themselves (originally intended as a communal roof garden). The general kitchen, the office and the servants' quarters were on the ground floor. Access and circulation was by means of cantilevered open galleries reached from either end by stairs. Bathrooms and kitchens were placed so as to intervene between bed-sitting rooms, reducing disturbance between tenants. Each flat had built-in light fittings, a sliding table, divan, wash basin, dressing table, electric cooker, sink and drainer and refrigerator. The services included central heating, dusting, bedmaking, shoe polishing and delivered meals.

The monolithic structure was in reinforced concrete, probably the first example in Britain of its use for domestic building on this scale. The external walls were 4" thick between pillars with an inch of cork insulation on the inner face which was used as permanent shuttering. The exterior finish was two coats of waterproofed and cream-tinted cement wash, applied direct to the concrete. Dividing partitions between the flats were of pumice concrete; the dividing partitions within were of 2" patent metal lathing, plastered. The flooring was a patent lino-like flooring in special tints laid on a pumice aggregate screed. On the sloping site the building was angled to the road to provide a south-west aspect for nearly all the living rooms, and so as to leave room for a garage in the north-east angle where cars could easily draw in.

In September 1946 Lawn Road was senselessly awarded second prize in a competition for the 'ugliest building' run by the magazine *Horizon*. Only twelve years before *The Architect and Building News* had written: 'Taking the building as a whole it is probably safe to call it the best example London can yet show of the modern school of design. Here continental influence is not an overlay or a mere badge of modernity; it has taken root and grown into a well reasoned and sensitive design.'[3]

Lawn Road should be remembered in the words of Nikolaus Pevsner: 'a milestone in the introduction of the modern movement into London'.[4]

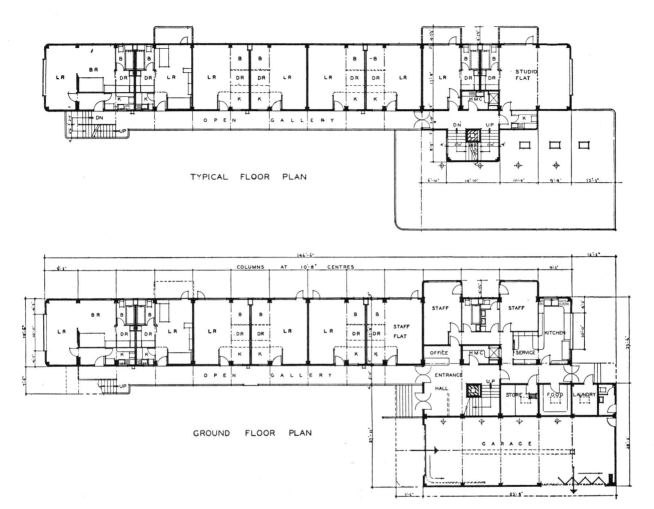

TYPICAL FLOOR PLAN

GROUND FLOOR PLAN

Typical floor plan

EMBASSY COURT FLATS 1935

'Embassy Court represents the new idea in seaside architecture. It is designed to catch the maximum sun and seaside air, and the elevation seems to be the inevitable surface result of this idea carried into practice.'[1]

The building stands 'a cool and haughty stranger' amongst the post-regency and Victorian hotels of Hove sea front. It was designed by Wells Coates in recognition of the demand for communal residences by the wealthier classes, who were finding the upkeep of the traditional large private house increasingly difficult.[2] *Building* reported in November 1935: 'The completion of the eleven-storey block of residential flats in Brighton marks an important stage in the development of the sea front of a popular English holiday resort. It definitely expresses a modern phase of English domestic life in terms of building in a manner indicative of structural principles essentially in tone with present-day scientific and economic development.'[3] The article went on to discuss the achievement of a 'subjective beauty . . . because it is unself-conscious and forthright in its fearless conception and handling'. Yet a functional beauty was also attained through the reproduction horizontally of plan units floor upon floor, from the necessity to provide each tenant with equal amenities.

The building is on a corner site and the L-shaped plan was conceived to give all living rooms and principal bedrooms an outlook over the sea. Each of these rooms opened onto a veranda and had access to a 'sun room'. On the ground floor were five flats and a banking room. 'The main entrance, sheltered externally by a large reinforced concrete marquise, has two pairs of doors, each centrally placed in a metal and glass screen. The metal work is cellulosed terra-cotta colour; the handles are covered with synthetic resin and held by silver-bronze brackets. The kicking-plates are also of silver-bronze.'[4]

Floors 1-8 comprised seven flats, the largest produced by the angle of the L-shape. Floors 9 and 10 comprised small recessed flats with terraces. The top floor was a sun-terrace with a cantilevered shelter. The basement provided space for garaging, heating equipment and stores.

The monolithic structure of reinforced concrete was originally designed to use a diagonal beam grid, which had been used on the continent to give a continuous floor of minimum thickness. But the system was not accepted by the local authorities. Coates and his engineers overcame the problem by creating a series of lattice stanchions, linking up the three pairs of lift shafts, their adjoining walls, the staircase towers and the end walls. The floors spanned the stanchions along central wall beams immediately supported on light columns. This avoided the use of projecting beams. The walls were 4½" thick, lined internally with cork and finished with a ¼" coat of plaster; the outside was finished with a ½" of light cream rendering. The steel windows had sills of glazed-tile, and the floors were part solid concrete (in which heating coils were embedded) and part hollow tile.

Coates designed furniture specifically for the show flats and his passion for 'unity of design' was apparent throughout the building: 'The architect has realised the value of plain surfaces and masses as an aid to restfulness and the achievement of a modern feeling in the rooms. Much thought has been given to the fitment and fittings: to the specially designed electric fires, the built-it wardrobes and lavatory fittings in the bedrooms, and the electric cooker and refrigerator and storage space in the kitchen.'[5]

Unfortunately the block soon became an embarrassment because of its constructional failures and high maintenance cost.

View from the seafront

PALACE GATE FLATS 1939

Palace Gate Flats, built for Randal Bell, were the first example of the 3-2 section in Britain. The principle was to have two living rooms the equivalent of three bedrooms, so that two complete flats occupied three floors of the building with access from every third floor only. Coates realised the limitations of designing in plan and had for some time been 'planning in section', for which he had identified three conditions: first, a more economical type of access other than open galleries on every floor; second, a living room which had a higher ceiling but would not add significantly to the volume and increase the overall cost; third, flexibility in the use of bedrooms and bathrooms, so that the size of the flats could vary without structural alterations. The experimental work on the continent by Scharoun and Ginsburg using a 2-1 section did not fulfil Coates's condition of flexibility, which he achieved at Palace Gate by alternating living rooms with bedrooms so that the '3-2 unit'

Sectional perspective

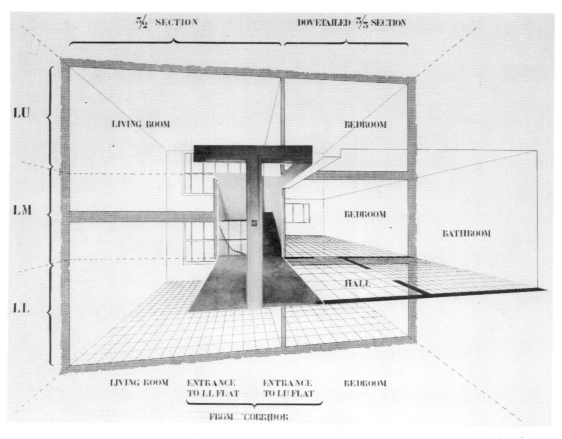

View from the garden side, exposing the 3-2 section

appeared in cross section and longitudinal section. Therefore the two bedrooms on the middle level could now be used separately: one for each of the adjoining flats, one for one of the flats only, or together or independently to form an additional two-room flat.

To make the most economical use of the corner site a 'T'-plan was devised; the main block to the east incorporating the '3-2 units' was linked by the lift shafts and staircase to the smaller block which was conventionally planned with a two-roomed flat per floor.

Below, the basement, serviced by two ramps one either side of the entrance, provided parking for twenty cars. The ground floor incorporated the entrance foyer, two flats and the staff accommodation. The three levels above represent the 'planning unit' on which the 3-2 system was used. On the top floor was a penthouse and roof terrace covered by a pergola of concrete beams. In total the building

consisted of twenty-seven dwellings. Each flat was
serviced by a thermostatically controlled central
heating system fed by an automatic plant in the
basement, fuelled on pulverised coal. The double
height living rooms had their heating facilities supple-
mented by open fire places, which burnt solid fuel
delivered to the flat in ready packed cartons.
Bathrooms and kitchens had a mechanical ventilating
system and were fully furnished.

The rent ranged from £175 for the flats in the
western annexe to £425 for a four bedroomed flat
in the main block.

Construction was of reinforced concrete with an
external permanent shuttering of precast artificial
stone slabs, whose origin Randal Bell explains in his
essay. On the interior face of the panel walls was a
2" cavity containing insulation and the horizontal
pipe runs and an internal wall of foamed slag blocks.
The floor construction was of hollow tile below
which was a 5/8" insulating slab with a plaster finish
for the ceiling. Above was a 1½" screed containing
the piped conduits and over which compressed cork
parquet was laid, except in the carpeted bedrooms.
The structure, designed by Samuely and Hamaan, was

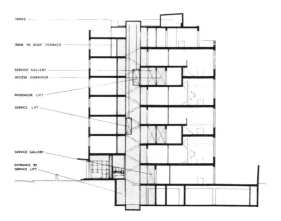

Cross section

contrived to avoid downstand beams except along
the permanent wall lines in order to maintain flush
ceilings and achieve minimum headroom.

Palace Gate in its
urban surroundings

49

HOUSE AT BENFLEET 1937

The house at Benfleet was built as a week-end residence for John Wyborne. It was situated on a steeply wooded site overlooking the Thames estuary, and to take advantage of the view Coates chose to raise all the principal rooms on to the first floor, except for the third bedroom and the main entrance hall.

The plan, designed within a square, was divided symmetrically with dining room and sitting room separated from the bedrooms by the kitchen and landing, which opened into the living room and bedroom via sliding screens. The main entrance, behind a glazed trellis screen and situated in the heart of the building, was surrounded by an open terrace. Service access was by way of an open stair to the first floor balcony, which was continued at the opposite end to create a shaded roof terrace.

Construction was of reinforced concrete external walls and floors. The roof was a concrete slab covered with 1″ cork flooring felt and cedar slats, and the internal finishes were mainly plaster and cork tiled floors.

The influence of Le Corbusier's Villa Savoye at Poissy, built eight years earlier, can be seen both in this house and in the house at Esher.

Ground and first floor plans divided symmetrically with dining room and living room separated from two bedrooms by the kitchen and staircase

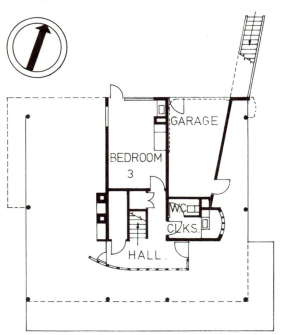

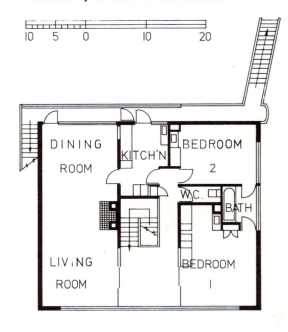

View of the south elevation from the garden

HOUSE AT ESHER 1939

'The Homewood' was designed by Patrick Gwynne for his father Commander Gwynne in association with Wells Coates, replacing a Victorian house in the grounds of a ten-acre site.

Coates had suggested a much enlarged 'Sunspan type' house, but the proposal was rejected by Commander Gwynne and his son Patrick, who had recently joined Coates's office. Patrick Gwynne's own design for a two-storey house was brought into the office under the terms of their associateship. The ground floor consisted of the garage, part of the service accommodation, an open terrace, the study, and the entrance hall, which had a spiral stair to the first floor. The first-floor rooms were divided into two wings at right angles to each other and linked by the staircase block. The larger wing contained the living room, dining room and kitchen with an

extension for the staff accommodation. The building was positioned in a wooded corner of the site affording the best view. Gwynne wanted to produce a 'country house' where the planning was informal, of modern materials. 'The house', writes Gwynne, 'is not really a Wells job; although he certainly influenced the final result, and there is quite a bit of him in it.'[1]

The use of brickwork on the ground floor may suggest a continuation of English tradition, but in the main the building owes much of its inspiration to Le Corbusier's concept of the structural frame emphasised at Villa Savoye in 1929, with the same

View from the wooded garden

The living room (facing south) looking towards
the dining room

slender columns and large strip windows. 'The design
of this house', wrote *The Architectural Review*,
'represents a remarkably thorough exploration of the
aesthetic and practical possibilities latent in the
application of new techniques to old problems of
the country house.'[2]

'Discarding the worn-out husk of "style" and the principle of "decorated structure" modern architecture postulates a coincidence of form and purpose.'[1]

MARS

The Modern Architectural Research (MARS) Group was formulated following a meeting on 28 February 1933 between the architects Wells Coates, Maxwell Fry and David Pleydell-Bouverie and the writer and critic Morton Shand. Coates had received a letter from Siegfried Giedion, Secretary to the International Congresses of Modern Architecture (CIAM), inviting him to form a British group of architects and engineers which would be allied to the national movements organised in nineteen other countries. Principally MARS existed to discuss and research contemporary problems and to present 'an architecture founded upon actuality, upon the pattern of our daily life'.[2]

Members included architects, engineers and writers, and by select recruitment the group came almost wholly to represent the British Modern Movement, whose concrete buildings and social policies became evident in schools, factories, shops, and housing all over Britain. Among its members in 1938, as well as the founders, were Ove Arup, John Betjeman, Geoffrey Boumphrey, Marcel Breuer, Hugh Casson, H.T. Cadbury-Brown, Serge Chermayeff, Amyas Connell, Elizabeth Denby, Joseph Emberton, Frederick Gibberd, Erno Goldfinger, Walter Gropius, Hubert de Cronin Hastings, Arthur Korn, Berthold Lubetkin, Colin Lucas, Raymond McGrath, László Moholy-Nagy, Raymond Mortimer, Herbert Read, J.M. Richards, Godfrey Samuel, Felix Samuely, Richard Sheppard, John Summerson, Cyril Sweet, Ralph Tubbs, Basil Ward, and F.R.S. Yorke.

The second MARS Group exhibition, 1938: layout plan

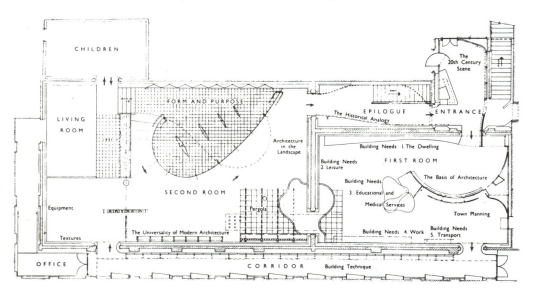

layout plan

The group studied town planning, mass production, standardisation, prefabrication, scientific research into new materials and new structures: ways of harnessing modern science to human needs. Following encouragement from CIAM, MARS organised two exhibitions at the New Burlington Galleries in London. At the first, in 1937, the public were invited 'to see, to touch, to compare and to judge of the real nature of modern architecture and the part it will play in modern life'.[3]

The second exhibition, entitled 'New Architecture', held in January 1938, embodied a spirit of optimism in the face of the worsening political situation in Europe: 'It is one of the purposes of this exhibition to emphasise that the modern movement is essentially a method of approach and not a crystallised "style" ...If...an architect's sympathies draw him into line with the modern movement, the passage of the idea from its first adumbration to the final design becomes a creative process, not one of mere intellectual compromise. With each successive step he widens his own experience of form and enlarges the boundaries of the movement to which he belongs.'[4]

Coates worked for MARS through the whole of its existence until its dissolution in the 1950s.

Le Corbusier talking to Wells Coates at CIAM 6, Bridgwater, 1947

CIAM — Les Congrès Internationaux d'Architecture Moderne — was founded in Switzerland in June 1928 when architectural delegates from many national groups met to discuss a programme of 'new architecture'. Le Corbusier and Siegfried Giedion, who were largely responsible for the preparation of the initial programme, were joined by such figures as Walter Gropius, Arthur Korn, Eric Mendelsohn and Mies van der Rohe from Germany, Alvar Aalto from Finland, Gregor Paulsson from Sweden, Ernesto Rogers and Enrico Peresutti from Italy, J.L. Sert from Spain, Richard Neutra from the United States, and Andre Lurçat and Eugène Freyssinet from Paris. For some thirty years CIAM remained a mouthpiece for the Modern Movement and the International Style.

Corbusier, the most romantic of rationalists, wrote of CIAM as follows. 'CIAM is made up of architects and town planners from all the five continents; troublesome fellows with independent minds, who have been working and meeting together for twenty-three years. Inspired by a common faith and determination they offer you a solution: build up again good fellowship amongst yourselves, take an active part at the core of our rapidly changing world.'[5] CIAM members believed that in the works of modern architecture they would witness 'the gradual broadening of the architect's vision towards the ultimate realisation that structural science and an exact analysis of social needs can supply a sufficient basis for the creation of an architecture of universal applicability'.[6]

The first formal British delegation to CIAM was in 1933, when Geoffrey Boumphrey, Wells Coates, Godfrey Samuel, and F.R.S. Yorke went as MARS delegates to the Fourth Congress in Athens, taking with them their first analytical plans for London. Coates remained the principal British delegate for many years and was responsible for drafting many of the programmes that formed the basis of the CIAM congresses.

The CIAM congresses from 1929 to 1959 were concerned with formulating architectural ideals: they wanted to satisfy human needs for 'living, working, circulation, and recreation' (as stated in the Athens Charter, 1933). After the war members came from all over the world; they worked to provide places and buildings where people could live full lives — or as Wells Coates would have said, 'become all that they might have been'.

Wells Coates with Enrico Peresutti, Monica Pidgeon,
and Jean-Jacques Honegger at CIAM 8, Hoddesdon,
1951

CANADIAN PROJECTS

IROQUOIS NEW TOWN 1952-54

Visiting Canada in 1951, Coates heard of Iroquois,
a small town that was to be flooded by the St
Lawrence Seaway project. Here he conceived a new
town on the fine lakeside site which could be made
available, with mixed rather than one-industry
development coming from British as well as Canadian
sources. He prepared an ambitious scheme which
would allow for a population of 40,000 (the original
inhabitants numbered only 1,100). In 1952 he
returned twice to Canada and had his proposal agreed
in principle, being appointed planning consultant by
the Iroquois Municipal Council. The following
January Coates presented a pilot plan to the
Department of Planning and Development (Province
of Ontario); finding the scheme too big for them to
handle, they passed it on to the Ontario Hydro
Electric Commission, and the Commission's own
more modest plan, which included a major road
through the middle of the town, was eventually
adopted by the Government of Ontario in 1954.
Bitterly disappointed, Coates abandoned the scheme.

VANCOUVER FLATS 1957

In Vancouver Coates developed the 3-2 section used
in 1939 at Palace Gate, proposing a 17-storey block
of flats on a Y-shaped plan. Each arm lay at 120°️ to
the others so that the principal rooms had an east,
west, south-east or south-west aspect.

Access to the flats was on every third floor
reached from the lift shafts and staircase of the
central core. Beneath the first floors of the arms, the
space was left open to provide car parking with the
entrance hall, office and shops on the ground floor
of the centre block. Although planned for two
suitable sites, one on the Vancouver Peninsula and
the other overlooking Horseshoe Bay, the project
never developed and remained on the drawing board.

MASS RAPID TRANSIT 1957

On 2 July 1957 Coates signed a six-month agreement
with the British Columbia Electric Company, to
investigate mass rapid transit systems. Coates's
36-page report opened with an analysis of existing
rapid transit schemes and included a page on
'miniaturisation' which assessed minimum space
requirements for travelling passengers. The report
concluded with Coates's own solution, the Monospan
Twin-Ride system, which carried an aluminium alloy
vehicle on either side of an I-beam supported on
columns. B.C. Electric were not empowered to enter
such fields of development, but they offered to
support the system if a developer could be found.
Further investigation by a developer in New York
proved the project to be impractical, as the engineer
J. Breen wrote: 'It would seem that the structure
and cost necessary to provide safety and durability
would eliminate a great part of the value of this
system.'[1]

Aerial view of Iroquois showing the shoreline before
and after flooding (broken white line)

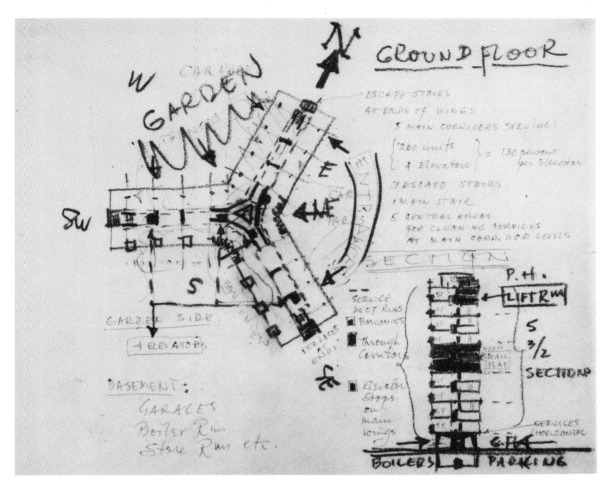

Plan and section from Coates's sketchbook

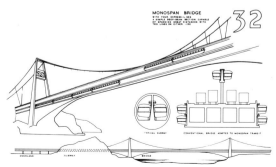

Report on Mass Rapid Transit Systems for B.C.
Electric Company: Monospan Bridge

Coates, who had a passion for the sea, designed and built 'Blue Mix' and launched her in 1939. The 14′ speed boat was constructed of 24-gauge mild steel, cold rolled into dovetail corrugated sheet (an idea developed from the Sunspan House of 1934) fixed to a wooden frame, and coated with a hard setting rubber-latex based plastic. He presented the prototype to the Admiralty, who became interested in its potential as a lightweight mass-produced craft. Unfortunately it was destroyed by an air raid whilst in storage.

Not long after this, however, Coates began work on a more ambitious project for a cruising yacht which was to have a revolutionary rig, the 'Wingsail'. Both his knowledge of the Chinese junk rig (seen during his boyhood in Japan) and his experience of aerodynamics during the Second World War furnished him with ideas towards improving

Wells Coates sailing 'Fey Loong'

contemporary sail design. The Wingsail took an exact aerofoil curve, making the greatest use of the 'high-lift' area along the leading edge of the sail, while keeping its total area to a minimum; this reduced the angle of heel and presented the most efficient profile to the water. The streamlined mast extended over the leading edge of double thickness sail, seen in cross section as the letter Y and stiffened by horizontal battens. This ensured as little a break as possible between mast and sail, avoiding turbulence on the leading edge. To further its efficiency Coates included a central pivot in the boom, which enabled an arching control to trim the sail to the shape of a bird's wing.

A small prototype model of the 16′ 'Wingsail Catamaran' was completed in 1946 and exhibited at the Britain Can Make It Exhibition. The actual Wingsail Catamaran was launched in 1948 and trials took place on the Norfolk Broads. The rig was successful: it sailed closer to the wind than the conventional Bermuda rig.

Coates was encouraged to continue work on his dream yacht, the yawl 'Fey Loong', where he developed his ideas for the interior and made a number of refinements to the Wingsail rig. Originally designed to accommodate eight, the scheme proved too costly and in 1950 was modified to sleep six in order to suit the standard Santander hull designed by J. Laurent Giles.

'Fey Loong' was launched on the Thames in 1954 and sailed in light winds in the Solent, but opportunities for trials were few. In 1955, when Coates was appointed Visiting Professor at the University of Harvard, 'Fey Loong' was put into storage, never to be sailed by her designer again. Wells Coates moved from Harvard to Vancouver, where in 1958 he suffered a fatal heart attack.

The Wingsail Catamaran sailing on the Norfolk Broads, 1948

PANEL 2

1 Wells Coates, 'Materials for Architecture', *The Architects' Journal*, 4 November 1931.
2 Wells Coates, 'Planning in Section', *The Architectural Review*, August 1937.
3 Ibid.
4 Ibid.
5 Ibid.

PANEL 3

1 Derek C. Wheatley, 'Economy in Shop Fittings', *The Shoe and Leather Record*, 13 February 1931.
2 ' "Modern" Shop-Front Design', *The Cabinet Maker and Complete House Furniture*, 3 January 1931.
3 Ibid.

PANELS 4 & 5

1 *Radio Times*, 13 May 1932.
2 *The Architects' Journal*, 7 September 1932, p. 279.
3 *Wells Coates: A Monograph*, Gordon Fraser, London, 1978, p. 36.

PANEL 6

1 'Craftsman's Portfolio', *The Architectural Review*, July 1932.
2 Ibid.
3 Wells Coates, 'Furniture Today — Furniture Tomorrow', *The Architectural Review*, July 1932.
4 Geoffrey Boumphrey, 'The Designers. 6. Wells Coates', Decoration Supplement to *The Architectural Review*, August 1932.

PANEL 7

1 'Materials for Architecture', *The Architects' Journal*, 4 November 1931.
2 'Furniture Today — Furniture Tomorrow', *The Architectural Review*, July 1932.
3 Open University Radio-vision. The History of Architecture and Design 1890-1939 — 'The Work of Isokon'. Written and read by Jack Pritchard, 25 June 1974.

PANEL 8

1 *Tottenham Sentinel*, 4 October 1934.
2 Paul L. Smith, 'Plastics in the Home', *Decoration*, August 1936.

PANEL 9

1 *The Architects' Journal*, 11 March 1931.
2 'The Architect's Portfolio No 230', *The Architect and Building News*, 29 September 1933.
3 Wells Coates, 'Planning the Festival of Britain Telekinema', *British Kinematography*, Vol 18 No 4, 8 October 1950.

PANEL 10

1 *The Architectural Review*, 25 March 1937.

PANEL 11

1 Memorandum to Graham Maw, July 1932, quoted in Sherban Cantacuzino, *Wells Coates*.
2 Morton Shand, 'The Sunspan House Olympia', *The Architects' Journal*, 26 April 1934.
3 'Room Units' Report, Wells Coates Associates, April 1947, Laura Cohn archives.
4 Wells Coates letter to Gordon Russell, 1 August 1946, quoted in Sherban Cantacuzino, *Wells Coates*.
5 'Room Units' Report, April 1947.

PANELS 12 & 13

1 Quoted in Sherban Cantacuzino, *Wells Coates*, p. 52.
2 *The Times*, 4 August 1934.
3 *The Architect and Building News*, 10 August 1934.
4 Quoted in Edward Carter, 'The Social/Architectural Background', *Hampstead in the Thirties*, exhibition catalogue, 1974.

PANELS 14 & 15

1 'Embassy Court, Brighton', *Building*, August 1934.
2 'Embassy Court, Brighton', *Building*, November 1935.
3 Ibid.
4 'Embassy Court, Brighton – 1', *The Architect's Portfolio*, No 318.
5 'Embassy Court, Brighton', *Building*, November, 1935.

PANEL 18

1 Patrick Gwynne, letter to Laura Cohn, 5 April 1979.
2 ' "The Homewood" Esher, Surrey', *The Architectural Review*, September 1939.

PANEL 19

1 'New Architecture', MARS Exhibition, New Burlington Galleries, 11-29 January 1938, catalogue, p. 18.
2 Ibid., p. 10.
3 Modern Architecture Exhibition, MARS, New Burlington Galleries, June 1937, cover of catalogue.
4 'New Architecture', catalogue, p. 6.
5 *The Heart of the City*, ed. J. Tyrwhitt et al, Lund Humphries, 1952, p. xii.
6 'New Architecture', catalogue, p. 5.

PANEL 20

1 J. Breen to Coates, 9 April 1958, quoted in Sherban Cantacuzino, *Wells Coates.*

WELLS COATES
by Randal Bell

I met Wells by chance at one of those densely crowded cocktail parties of the mid 'thirties.

'What do you do?' I shouted. 'I design buildings', he yelled. 'Really! I build them', I trumpeted. 'We should get together', he roared. 'But we can't talk here!'

And so it was that I visited 18 Yeoman's Row about a week later. Our first conversation covered a wide range of subjects and we discovered a mutual interest in sailing and motor cars, as well as our fundamental predilection to building design.

I was fascinated by the design of 18 Yeoman's Row, and on taking my leave almost casually said, 'Why cannot you do something like this for flat dwellers?'

Thus it was that Wells brought to my office a model of the 3-2 section, and this first serious business meeting was unforgettable and slightly funny. We spent an hour or so on the model, and with his aid I grasped the implications of design in section. The next hour was spent in assessing the site he proposed at 10 Palace Gate — how many flats could be built, and all the usual financial implications, at the end of which I said, 'All right, I'll build it'. Wells went very pale (for a moment I thought he was going to fall off his chair) and said in a weak voice 'Do you mind saying that again?' 'I'll build it', I repeated, and so it transpired.

At that moment I did not know Wells particularly well nor he me, but there followed upon this meeting a period of intense activity for us both.

Working with Wells was refreshing. He would daily produce drawings for me to see and we met each evening to pull them about until both of us were fully satisfied. My daytime was occupied with settling finance, contracting, planning approvals, and so forth, in which he took no part. Between us, all was done and the contractor was on site 'cutting the first sod' (which actually was felling the old Lithuanian Embassy building) just six weeks after our first business meeting.

Our relationship became more mature as work at 10 Palace Gate progressed, and I found myself having to argue. It started when he wanted to finish the building in concrete, which I vetoed absolutely on grounds of crazing, and maintenance — to keep a concrete building looking clean and crisp involves constant (and expensive) attention. We both wanted stone, which was 'out' on grounds of cost and weight, and although two or more elevations were prepared with brick cladding, neither of us liked them.

At such moments I discovered Wells could be counted on to surface at his best. He produced a highly ingenious form of cladding in artificial stone slabs, which obviated the need for scaffolding and was all right for weight. It meant that an artificial stone-faced building could be gained for the same price as brick panels. There has never, perhaps, been given enough attention to this experiment. In the event it was not quite perfect, because we were working nearer to engineering limits than builders' tolerances. But with some modification this system could be the perfect answer, particularly in tight city situations where buildings are crowded, if a stone-faced exterior were the need.

I also had to insist that metal windows were put into teak sub-frames, but I had no real resistance to this request. More frequently I had to quash improvements which Wells wanted to introduce in the course of building. Here my refusals would make him very cross, but I would tell him that as I was a developer working to a schedule of time and money, all such improvements must wait until the next building came along.

With Wells it was necessary for the financing client to know his subject, otherwise Wells would run ahead always improving and altering, which could prove to be a very expensive matter.

An example of his love of innovation at Palace Gate was the adoption of a new form of boiler. This sounded fine and I accepted it, although it was experimental. It burnt 'talcum powder' fine coal dust which was delivered to a hopper and then a worm-screw drive fed this dust to a burner where it was combusted with the assistance of an air jet. After its installation I received more and more complaints about powder dust from adjoining owners, and I personally examined the dust under the microscope when it was at once apparent that there were uncombusted particles which amounted to tiny pieces of clinker.

10 Palace Gate is the only positive evidence of our relationship, but between 1936 and 1939 we worked on many projects of which little or no evidence now remains.

My personal ambition at this period was to find a way to make slum clearance commercially viable, and in this purpose I found an eager collaborator in Wells. We spent many hours together testing methods, the upshot of which was that the minimal site size to make any such scheme feasible was four acres — a formidable size indeed in the London area, particularly when it needed to be square or only slightly oblong in shape.

Nothing daunted, I found the owners of land bounded roughly by Tottenham Court Road, the back of Oxford Street, Goodge Street, and Charlotte Street (or a little beyond), and was permitted to search. I decided that as I was busy all day I would work from 5 p.m. to 8 p.m. and find out how the land lay piecemeal. The result was immediate. Within forty-eight hours I was known by sight to every tart in the area, who once they realised that I was not 'from the landlord' nor seeking their professional services, accepted my presence with an open-handed candour, telling me all they knew of the locality (which, as it happened, was plenty!).

In the back streets I discovered an abundance of small workshops in which products using meticulous crafts and engineering skills were prepared and passed to larger contractors.

In closely built slum property, a builder has to 'break in' and demolish some old buildings so as to lay first foundations, drains, and so on for the new and larger buildings. The problem is to avoid displacing people from their homes before new ones are ready. It soon became apparent to me that the complication of gaining sufficient space for a break in for development was too much, and I abandoned my search.

Wells had no part in this exercise, though he was fully informed by me of the curious, sometimes bawdy, and commercially complicated problems which arose from my investigation.

We both were faced with the problem of how to break into a slum clearance site. It was in late 1937 that I found an ideal prospect. Beaumont Estate in Stepney was a group of 750 houses — 'without a bathroom amongst them' as I described it. On this Wells produced drawings for a redevelopment scheme which was to prove what had now become a mutual theory, that on suitable areas (provided they were not less than 4 acres) we could make slum clearance actually pay!

With his usual brilliance when faced with a challenge, he sited the first buildings in a street so that no question of a break in arose. This is where my search in the West End site bore fruit. From that we had both realised that gaining and demolishing buildings without first having the alternative accommodation at call would make any scheme unworkable.

In financial analysis the slum clearance scheme worked. I had at command all the finance necessary. The costs of the redevelopment would have involved the Estate in borrowing; but allowing for that, the Estate annual income would have been more than doubled, this not because of rent increases, but because at the same or similar low rents the increase in the number of persons housed made up the difference.

We both felt that our point had been made. Alas, the Estate deferred decision. The political scene was sinister, Czechoslovakia was under threat, and its reluctance to embark on a three-year project was understandable. By the time it came up for review the political scene was worse. Nothing happened! Shortly afterwards we put on our uniforms and went our ways.

Not all our time in those three short years before the war were spent in intensive work on buildings. For example: I visited Tufton Manor one week-end with my wife. A cow bellowed *but immediately* underneath our bedroom window all night, but it was nevertheless a blissful week-end.

We sailed and fished at Shaldon in Devon and designed sails for my 16 footer. Once we were invited to lunch at the Imperial Hotel, Torquay by a friend staying there. Wells and I were sailing to try out some change of rig, and fish for mackerel at the same time. The wind headed and it was obvious that we could not get back in time to change and motor over for our lunch. 'Sail to Torquay', cried Wells, and so we did, squelching into the hotel in our sailing clothes, and presenting our host with two very dead mackerel hooked on our journey.

It was on 19th October 1945 that in battle dress and bush hat, clutching my cardboard box containing my dreadful civilian suit, I left Olympia and made my way to Marylebone Station. I was waiting at the lights where Melcombe Street meets Dorset Square when who should draw up but Wells driving his Lancia.

This coincidence left us both flabbergasted but delighted, and I resumed my journey to Northampton-shire with an added pleasure, for not only was I returning home but had met a particular friend en route! Wells came to visit us at Helmdon where I was living, and long discussions ensued as to where we might be able to pick up the threads of our prewar activities.

The immediate post-war period was a particularly difficult time for us both. Although we were in close contact nothing bore fruit. The opportunities were not there. Lack of materials and building restrictions made building speculatively at best totally hazardous, and more usually downright impossible. We thought about flat pack tubular furniture but material obstacles came in the way of manufacture.

I was an interested commentator on Wingsail design, and although I had no real hand in its production, some of my suggestions related to handling characteristics and running gear and I like to think were useful. Wells, as always, was critically interested in what I had to say. It was a feature of our relationship that with complete contentment we

could tear any of his designs apart, his platform being to argue the structural and aesthetic merits, mine the functional and commercial aspects.

So it was with Room Units, where I was not interested in Rooms in a Frame for UK and European use. I thought that the system would prove too expensive, and the idea of a building which became 'toothless', so to speak, at week-ends did not appeal to me. Rooms in a Garden, however, did appeal very much.

For the first time post-war Wells and I were able to join forces at St Lawrence Cliffs Hotel at Ramsgate, Kent — a project started by two hotel experts, Sydney Stacey and Felix Schreyeck, MBE. Wells converted the old house to an hotel with perforce a limited number of bedrooms, later to be increased by Room Units. There was not the money to be elaborate, but what he did was vividly effective.

Sydney Stacey told me that at a place like Ramsgate you put a bed of scarlet geraniums along the frontage, which kept away the common herd (who passed it saying 'posh place') — but instantly attracted the Rolls and Bentley owners.

After the opening five of us played poker before going to bed — for tiny stakes. Nobody had made or lost much when we rounded off our evening with a 'cold flop' for a kitty into which we had all put a shilling. Wells was the dealer — round went the cards face up finishing with an ace for the dealer. Next time round he had 2, then 3, 4, 5, *in that order,* and so the day ended with yet another of Well's incredible coincidences, which was of course suitably celebrated!

The geraniums grew, but the Rolls and Bentley owners cannot have passed that way, for the hotel failed.

The final endeavour was Iroquois New Town, which Wells regarded as an opportunity for British impact in Canada — the skills and experience of the one combining with the space and natural resources of the other. In 1953, so as to establish a development corporation, a syndicate was formed consisting of Wells, architect, myself, surveyor, my brother, barrister, and F.T. Wright, City chartered accountant.

My brother and I had discussions at board level with City merchant bankers, who strongly advised us to seek our finance in Canada. Meanwhile, Wells introduced a principal who (we thought) was negotiating with an important Canadian Assurance Company. When we found that his negotiations were in the City we did not think that he was likely to succeed. We told this to Wells, and said that we would support him if there was a fresh Canadian negotiation. Wells elected to go it alone, which ended my connection with the project.

The fact is that I never told Wells how I intended to finance Iroquois, although my brother and Wright both knew of and approved my ideas. Iroquois was to be inundated in toto, and part of the adjoining farmlands of Matilda were also to be flooded. The Iroquoits were numerous, but Matilda was held in only seven ownerships.

If I could establish that a Canadian institution would lend building finance and repayment mortages on new buildings, then the compensation which would have to be given would provide the necessary equities. As inevitably the Iroquoits would have to be housed on Matilda land I could negotiate with only seven owners of a vast farm territory, persuading them to grant land leases to the newcomers, making the whole decanting process simple and in the long term a benefit to the seven Matildats. It might have worked!

At this period Wells liked to be the 'alter ego' in all negotiations, and the reason I was withdrawn about my intentions in the finance of Iroquois was that I feared that if I told him he would rush off prematurely and prejudice success — for he had no experience of the financial negotiations I intended.

Shortly after this, Wells left England, selling to me his lovely Lancia before he went, and I saw him no more.

It has been said that Wells quarrelled with his friends. I never quarrelled with him. Throughout a long friendship with many ups and downs, there was always a close personal relationship which defied all storms.

After he left I had some cheerful letters from Canada and then one day, alas, news that he had died.

Freedom and Responsibility in the Experience of the Architect
by Wells Coates

Before an architect can begin to outline the shape of his contribution to this series of discussions, he may perhaps be allowed, in an introduction, to select a particular site and describe a general background for his remarks. I propose to start off with a sort of parable. My story is from a book by the Rev. J.H. Weeks, entitled *Among the Congo Cannibals*:

'I remember on one occasion (he writes) wanting the word for table. There were five or six boys standing around and, tapping a table with my fore-finger, I asked "What is this?"'

'One boy said it was a *dodela*, another that it was *etanda*, a third stated that it was *bokali*, a fourth that it was *elamba*, and the fifth said it was *meza*.

'These various words we wrote in our notebook, and congratulated ourselves that we were working among a people who possessed so rich a language that they had five words for one simple article.'

A short analysis of this apparently simple sign-and-word situation might have saved the reverend gentle-man the trouble of finding out later that

'One lad had thought we wanted the word for *tapping*; another understood we were seeking the word for the *material* of which the table was made; another had an idea that we required the word for *hardness*, another thought we wished for a name for that which *covered* the table; and the last, not being able, perhaps, to think of anything else, gave us the word *meza*, table — the very word we were seeking.'

The name of the 'experience of a table' was of course table, for ordinary purposes: it was also an expression or experience of tapping, etc. The answers were all to the point: so far as that point was defined. It seems to me that similar difficulties arise when one is asked 'What is architecture?' or 'What is the architect's place or relationship to society?' Mere opinions are made to take the place of technical investigation of visual and material scenes: or else technical facts are made to assume the role of critical values: so that discussion is impossible or even meaningless unless preceded by elaborate definitions of terms.

The apprehension and appreciation of *creative forms* in architecture — an art which in its *imitative* forms continues to uphold obsolete social, moral and even technical principles — becomes a difficult affair to set out in words. Let us begin by saying that the social characteristics of an age determine the characteristics of its art, and this is more so in architecture than in any other art. And by 'characteristics' we mean the diversity of form over and above the sameness of essential intention. The true tradition of art lies in its *essential intentions*.

What is this essential intention, in Architecture? Reduced to its simplest elements it is the provision of *ordered shelter* and *an aspect of significance* in the arrangement of buildings and the forms of nature in which they are placed. These buildings must cater for a multitude of human needs and activities. In this sense, architecture has always been the most direct, the most complete, expression of the culture of an age: the least personal, and the most objective of the arts. The whole complex of human impulses and attitudes — the needs, expectations, satisfactions, surprisals and disappointments — these are the first of the architect's raw materials.

Every change in human conditions brings with it possibilities of new relationships of human needs, and the necessity arises to order them anew, to give them form, freedom and fullness — the richness of life. Evidence of the necessity of a new order reveals itself every other day, in some new social or economic 'crisis'. As creative architects, we are concerned with a future which must be planned, rather than a past which must be patched up at all costs. And, more often than not, we find that the past is *not* all behind us: but out there in front blocking the way to the kind of future we can picture but not yet achieve. And blocking the way, moreover, in the most alarmingly durable building materials. Our inheritance of culture, and the majority of architectural forms in which it is contained, has not, perhaps, been discounted by death duties commen-surate with the real deadness of the encumbrances passed on to us.

In an age of ever-increasing specialisation, to be

a man of culture in Europe or America today, means so often merely to possess encyclopaedic information about one group of subjects: appreciation of other needs and activities is too often merely of a literary order. In the Far East it was not so at least until lately. The cultured man, there, is one who is himself an artist of living: who has been trained sensually to aesthetic apprehension: who inherits a culture perpetually resurrected in his own eyes, voice, hands and movements. It is fortunate for all of us that the effects, the functions, and the qualities of *all* the old architectures (in the plural), can be imagined, experienced, remembered or reconstructed in our minds. Never has detailed knowledge of this art been so expert, or so all-inclusive of world-culture. But, to respond to the old forms and materials, and to perceive their true intent *in their own age*, is to begin to understand the essential intention of the new architecture of today. To know the difference in value between a merely surprising trick, and a noble invention: to know what subtle combinations and resolution of human impulses make up the select values of an enclosed and habitable space; to know what are the ingredients in the making of that particular quality of 'residual repose' which buildings alone can possess, is to hold the essential intention of tradition in architecture. Paul Valéry said in his book *Eupalinos, or the Architect*:

'What is important for me above all else is to obtain from that which is going to be, that it should with all the vigour of its newness satisfy the reasonable requirements of that which has been . . . How can one help being obscure.'

Or again from Wyndham Lewis' *Caliph's Design*:

'The arrangement seems to be that you spend half your time destroying the cheap, the foolish, the repellent: and the other half enjoying what is left after your efforts.

'This evidently being how we are intended to live, there is no excuse for slackness in the carrying out of your unpleasant duty: that is, to desire equity, mansuetude, in human relations; to fight against violence; and to work for formal beauty, significance

and so forth, in the arrangement and aspect of life.'

How free in that field is the architect today, in the carrying out of his essential intentions; and where does his responsibility take him? Firstly, I think the architect must contrive to be quite free within himself. The 'black box' within his cranium must have a specially sensitive system of selectors and predictors, which enable him to discern significance where others see only disorder, and to allow him to be free to accept the ideas that come to him, and to interpret these into forms which will serve life. To this attainment, there are requisite also certain routines of knowledge, of imagination and of control: he must know a good deal about the workings of the *inside* of things: about *science*, the *identifier*, the measurer and calculator. And he must know, and feel, the science of the *outside* of things: he must be an artist: a *differentiator*, selector and maker.

In the routine practice of his art, like the conductor of an orchestra, the architect must first be free to select his instruments and his executants. He should, preferably, be practised in the art of a number of these instruments, and certainly must know how all of them should be played. He must ensure that the whole orchestra, including the soloists, the specialists, is playing in tune, and moreover, playing the same tune. And, as he is also the composer of the music to be played, in him is vested the freedom to identify, to differentiate, and to eliminate. Throughout the rehearsals he will be responsible for creating, together with the whole orchestra, the composition which will finally be performed.

Now this is all very well, you may be saying — but what about the programme, the requirements, the financial backing: indeed, what about the client? What I have been trying to outline is a kind of yard-stick with which we may measure the whole performance of architecture, which includes the client, the customer who pays for, and must use, the acts of this performance: and I see no reason why the highest standards of calibration should not be employed and set forth in these matters. It is indeed at this stage in the development of our thesis, that the first obstructions to freedom, and also the real responsibilities of the architect, are encountered.

Clients may be divided into several categories. Firstly the ideal client, the architect himself: or rather, we should say the architect without a client, from whose imaginative and fertile brain has sprung much of the truly inventive architecture of the world. Many of the revolutionary movements in architecture — structurally there have been indeed very few revolutions in our history — have derived from such an architect as Le Corbusier in our own day: he has influenced ten thousand times the number of clients he might have had, through the conveyance to other architects of a whole world of forms, and liberations from the pretences of other days, and ways of building. Such an architect may permit himself to say that a building is never finished until it has been torn down to make way for a better one.

The architect, if he is to be more than a practitioner or master-builder, will not accept the world as it is, and yet he will not deny its existence and live like a hermit, nor will he deny his primal responsibilities as an artist, to the social structure of which he is a part. He may, perhaps, have learned with Confucius that 'There are only the wise of the highest class, and the stupid of the lowest, who cannot be changed', and fortified with this cheerful thought, he will enter the world of action, neither accepting nor denying its structure, and sooner or later he will meet a client. If he is lucky, or lives in certain countries, he may meet a client of the old pattern, the patron of the arts, whose magic wand and illimitable purse allow the grandest or the wildest of conceptions to be realised.

Much of the best, and most of the really pretentious architecture in the world has resulted from such a conjunction of architect and patron in which freedom to realise forms is coupled on the one hand either with a complete assumption of responsibility to his fellow men in society; or on the other, without boundaries or limits of any kind, his freedom has expanded into expensive and irrelevant irresponsibility. But he is more likely to meet a client of quite a different sort: the man of perception, taste and talent who is possessed of a purse totally inadequate for his purpose. These are the sorry design-situations: freedom to express is in being, but not manifest, and the responsibility for the absence of realisation can never be pinned down. And again, he may meet a person whose precise purposes match the contents of his privy purse. The architect will be handed in diagrammatic form the total requirements for a building — it is only necessary for him to fill in the sordid building details: he is the building servant, he is expected to have no freedom, and little responsibility. Such people we call 'designing clients': they require careful handling.

The process whereby the operational requirements of private clients may be transformed into real structures and significant forms allow of every kind of variation, of every interplay between the parties, of their respective freedoms and responsibilities. Architects will agree that the most difficult task is the equating of his client's purposes not only to his purse, but also to the architect's own conception of architecture, his responsibilities towards his own ideas of the essential intentions of architecture towards society as a whole. If A, his purpose, does not equate to B, his purse, there are only two solutions: decrease A, or increase B. But if the purpose is not in alignment with his sense of responsibility, the architect is presented with an equation which is not immediately soluble. He may even be forced to decline the commission. Such a decision, especially for the young architect making his way, presents many difficulties, not the least of which is economic. His feeling of responsibility denies him the freedom to create; his freedom of choice determines that he shall not take on an impossible responsibility.

In the next category of client we may mention the group of persons, the executives of an industry, the Building Committee of a vast Authority: whose interests generally lie largely in the launching of a financial operation rather than in the placing of an architectural commission. In such situations, very great powers are wielded for good or for evil, architecturally speaking, and the architect's freedom is whittled down by an attendant group of specialists and 'know-how' men employed by the group-client, to whom he is expected to be a 'yes-man'. Thus, a part of the architect's responsibility devolves forever upon the shoulders of a vast, impersonal, calculating machine-like entity: architecture gives way to mere building: to the spending of millions in order that more millions shall be produced from the fabric of steel, concrete, wood and glass. Relationship, responsibility to other buildings and to society, or to the comfort and happiness of the people who will work or live in these structures, is not on the agenda at all. And unfortunately there are always practitioners in architecture and in building who will, irresponsibly, provide what men ignorantly and wrongly and antisocially desire for their own personal ends, or what they think will be good, or good enough, for others.

But I imagine a new light is beginning to shine, even amongst these vast constellations of big industry: it is beginning to be understood that the provision of *amenity* — to use a much abused current word — *for the people*, is itself a long-term financial operation: formal beauty, significance, in fact *architecture*, begins to pay big dividends: we are at the gates of a new road towards responsibility for architecture. Especially in the new and un-developed territories of the world it is beginning to be realised that mere encampments suitably adjacent to the huge plant — the so-called 'company-town' — are not adequate to retain the interest and thus the employment of the people in that place. Nor is it enough, they have discovered, to provide amusements, arrangements for pastimes and sports of all kinds: the natural beauty of the countryside and the landscape must be retained and enhanced in value by the moulding into it of an organic and integrated arrangement of buildings: man's *appointed place* for work and for living must be *in being* and made manifest: his natural instinct to found a family and to settle down there, must be invited, and richly fulfilled.

At the next stage of our saga of clients, the tendency for governments to step in and to make laws demanding the provision of 'amenities' for a free and full life is revealed. The essential intentions of architecture are faintly discernible here: the conditions wherein architects may be allowed to achieve freedom within a framework, a skeletal structure, of governmental *responsibility*, are everywhere beginning to be announced. In many ways, this country leads the world in this tendency: my colleagues from abroad frequently acknowledge this.

And so we come to the next stage in our thesis: the architect's responsibility in the contemporary scene expands from an interpretation of the necessities of what I term the 'select value of a personal environment' for a private client, to the social requirements of the day and age. These requirements outreach the building of single structures in the disordered and tortured muddle of contemporary city streets, which so many of us have had to be content to build: those tiny precedents or previews, for the architecture we know can only be realised in larger formations and sectors. So we move from 'postage-stamp' architecture, located upon choice nodal points of the map, to a collection of pictures: of streets and squares, of parks and parkways, of centres or 'cores' for community life: we move on to the conception of a new town. The ingredients or elements must be disposed: places for work, and for living; areas designed for the cultivation of the mind and body; all of these linked with systems of communication which command vehicles to be orderly instead of irresponsible; systems which ensure the re-establishment upon his private throne, of the Royal Pedestrian ('le royauté des piétons,' as Corbusier puts it). Given such responsibilities, the architect-planner will not misuse his new freedom. The tradition of architecture is to seek the order that leads to freedom and fullness of life. Architecture has to serve the purposes of the people, as well as the purposes of beauty: thus will it 'serve life'.

So in the new society which is evolving today, the architect finds himself in the most arduous, the most responsible of positions. Human possibilities have altered more in the past 100 years than they had in the previous 10,000. But *customs* change more slowly than conditions. To assume the survival of a dying society in order to bring once more to life what Lethaby called a 'pretence to beauty at second-hand' is to urge the continuance of a stupid and meaningless torture.

It is commonly assumed that most people know what they want to do with their lives. Our experience shows that this is not so: most people accept an existing pattern or framework, in which to live without assuming any responsibilities. They do not want revolution, or even evolution: but at the same time the architects find that if a new pattern is presented to them for inspection: a new and *articulate* pattern, the people naturally accept and begin to desire order and significance in the stage settings for their lives. The common lag of people lack the opportunity and the creative capacity to make for themselves, as they did in less complex, less specialised ages, the forms which serve life, and that applies to architecture and to everything they use every day. If the responsibilities of the contemporary architect to his final clients — the people as a whole — are to be fully shouldered, essential changes must be made in the form and composition of his orchestra. Mere taste, fashion, or precept cannot rule in this new domain. The sociologist, the economist, the psychologist, the biologist and the neurologist — all the new specialists in humanist advance through greater knowledge, through the making of new tools and instruments to assess and predict what people really need or want — all these must somehow be brought into the general playing area — the orchestra — of architecture: and assist in making the new compositions which society anxiously awaits.

Advances in techniques of construction of an entirely new order — the industrialisation of building techniques — must, on a global scale, be brought into play: the bigger the orchestra, the bigger the drums needed to keep time: so that the performance may equal the principle and the realisation match the new relationships between man and man, and nation and nation. If at any time in the history of mankind, all persons of high regard and intelligence had been bound to work together, the result would have been a prodigy of power for good. I believe that in such groupings as I have indicated — groupings of man's professions — between the new scientists of human advancement and the artists of architecture, a new and collective responsibility may arise, which will create the conditions for an architecture worthy of the mighty powers our society has at hand to wield. The wise of the highest class cannot be changed: maybe they need not be: they need only to consent to work together, to plough a common furrow through the barren fields of our inheritance, and therein to plant the seeds of a twentieth century classicism, a broadly based and democratic architecture, a society with the means, the tools, the instruments for personal freedom, and for the proper distribution of responsibility to all the people.

We have spoken of the new sense of responsibility evidenced by governments, in the advancement of laws for town and country planning, for amenity, for architecture. But I do not believe that the kind of freedom demanded by architecture can be achieved through the excessive compilation of rules and regulations. As Lao Tze said: 'When rules and regulations have multiplied, the world will be full of robbers and thieves.' There is a limit to the responsibilities which human nature can undertake freely, if petty restrictions undermine a general appetite for freedom.

I believe that the work of integrating, unifying, synthesizing a multitude of new human needs and appetencies — or perhaps I should say *unknown* needs — cannot be undertaken without the development of new means specifically designed to search and to research into the nature of man and his physical, mental and spiritual yearnings. Such means cannot be circumscribed within the narrow confines of a bureaucratic regime of rule and regulation, of forms and fancies. It has to be said that such formations as we see in this country, surrounding the concept of the New Towns, appear in many senses to be opposed to the very principle upon which they are designed to operate. An *apparent* freedom to create new towns is merely a smoke-screen for controls and obstructions which become at times irresponsible, negative, self-contradictory. Bureaucratic paper-forms and regulations can never keep step with the magnitude and speed of the changing problems of contemporary society: indeed these systems of administration are a definite obstruction to the freedom to undertake the development, and responsibility for the control, of human environment.

I believe that in this country, which invented the shape of democratic government for the world, the ways and means may be found to eliminate the over-load of bureaucracy which is obstructing progress everywhere: means to bring forward a new technique, a new modality of administration which will match in time and space the rapidly evolving order of society today. New centres of imaginative control, employing every resource which science may devise, must somehow be created to provide forms of environmental control commensurate with the scale of the problems of freedom of the individual and his responsibility to society in the contemporary world.

For the rest, an artist will seek *within himself* the freedom he needs, and the degree of responsibility he is prepared to shoulder.

1895	17 December. Born in Toyko, Japan
1913	World cruise from Japan to Vancouver on *SS Cleveland* Begins studies in Mechanical and Structural Engineering at McGill University College, Vancouver
1915-17	Joins Second Canadian Division of Field Artillery. To the front lines in France and Belgium
1918-19	Royal Naval Air Service, later Royal Air Force, scout pilot
1919-22	Returns to university in Vancouver, now University of British Columbia BA (1919) and BSc in Engineering (1922)
1922	Comes to London for post-graduate study Meets Maxwell Fry
1924	PhD (Engineering), London University Meets Marion Grove
1925	To Paris as journalist with *Daily Express* Develops interest in Le Corbusier's work Meets Alec Walker (textile designer) Arts Décoratifs exhibition
1927	Marries Marion Grove
1928	Crysede Silks, Cambridge. Shop 'Tayloroid' bow handles (D-handles) for Taylor, Pearce & Co Meets Jack and Molly Pritchard
1929	Cresta Silks Factory, Welwyn Garden City. Interior, furniture and fittings
1929-32	Cresta Shops. Interiors, furniture, and fittings Brompton Road, London; Bournemouth; Brighton; Bromley; Baker Street, London, Bond Street, London
1930	Lawn Road, Hampstead, London. Sketch plans for single house and linked houses Daughter Laura born
1931	Consultant designer to Isokon: bookcase units, Isotype houses
1931-35	Venesta exhibition stands
1932	Broadcasting House, London. Studios, furniture, light fittings and broadcasting equipment

34 Gordon Square, Bloomsbury, London. Conversion of flat
1 Kensington Palace Gardens, London. Conversion of flat
Partnership with David Pleydell-Bouverie
15 Elizabeth Street, London. Conversion of office
BBC Studios, Newcastle
Lawn Road, Hampstead, London. First project for flats
Wins E.K. Cole & Co (Ekco) competition for design of moulded wireless cabinet

1932-38	Furniture for Hilmor and PEL (Practical Equipment Limited)
1933	The 'minimum flat' exhibited at Dorland Hall Exhibition, London Stage set for Old Vic Theatre Company, London Member of Unit One Forms Modern Architectural Research (MARS) Group Delegate to CIAM 4 Congress, Athens
1934	Lawn Road, Hampstead, London. Flats Sunspan House, Daily Mail Ideal Home Exhibition (with David Pleydell-Bouverie) Elected FRIBA Unit One exhibition, Mayor Gallery, London
1934-38	Sunspan houses (with David Pleydell-Bouverie)
1934-46	Ekco wireless sets; television set; electric fires: AD 65; AD 36; AC 85; Radiogram; AC 76; AC 86; A 22; 'Radiotime'; 'Princess-Handbag'; TSC 113 television set; Thermovent heaters
1935	18 Yeoman's Row, Brompton Road, London. Conversion of studio flat for himself Embassy Court Flats, Brighton Separates from his wife Marion
1936	Hampden Nursery School, Holland Park, London. Conversion of interior Ekco Research Laboratories, Southend-

75

on-Sea, Essex
Meets Randal Bell
1936-39 Furniture for P.E. Gane and B. Burkle
1937 'Shipwrights', house at Benfleet, Essex
Slum Clearance Project, Bethnal Green, London
News Chronicle Schools Competition (with Denys Lasdun)
First MARS Group exhibition
CIAM 5 Congress, Paris
1938 MARS Group exhibition
1939 The Homewood, house in Esher, Surrey (Patrick Gwynne in association with Wells Coates)
10 Palace Gate, London. Flats
'Blue Mix' experimental dinghy
1939-45 Royal Air Force HQ Staff, in charge of unit controlling fighter aircraft development
1944 OBE (Military Class) for services to RAF
Appointed Royal Designer for Industry of the Royal Society of Arts
Seconded from RAF for 3 months to work as consultant to Aircraft Industries Research Organisation on Housing (AIROH)
1945 Resumes private practice in London
1946 Consultant to A.W. Hawksley Ltd of Gloucester on housing development
Wingsail Catamaran prototype model shown at Britain Can Make It Exhibition, London
Consultant designer for special version of De Havilland 'Dove' aircraft
1946-47 Room Unit Production project for standardised housing
1947 Daughter Laura returns to England from Canada
Designs for two aircraft interiors for BOAC

1948 CIAM 6 Congress, Bridgwater, Somerset
Wingsail Catamaran launched
Visits South America for A.W. Hawksley Ltd
1949 CIAM 7 Congress, Bergamo, Italy
Appointed President of CIAM Commission on Industrialised Building Techniques
Partnership with Jaqueline Tyrwhitt
1950 Consultant to Electrical and Mechanical Industries Ltd (EMI)
1951 Festival of Britain, South Bank, London: Telekinema; TV Pavilion; clocks for King and Queen
Work on final plans for 'Fey Loong' 30′ yawl, with J. Laurent Giles
Appointed Master of Faculty of Royal Designers for Industry
CIAM 8 Congress, Hoddesdon, Herts
1952-54 Project for Iroquois New Town, Ontario, Canada
1953 CIAM 9 Congress, Aix-en-Provence, France
1954 'Fey Loong' launched
1955 Visiting Critic in Architecture and Urban Design, Harvard University: summer term
1955-56 Visiting Professor of Architecture and Urban Design, Harvard Graduate School of Design
CAUSA, project for a Centre for Advanced and Unified Studies in the Applied Arts
1956 Returns to Vancouver
Project for flats, Ottawa
1957 Project for flats, Vancouver
Project '58 for downtown Vancouver, with group of Vancouver architects
First heart attack followed by 7 weeks in hospital
Consultant for British Columbia Electric Company, leading to project for the Monospan Twin-Ride System (MTRS)
1958 17 June. Death on beach at Vancouver